GWENNA]
John Wesley's An
A Cornish P.

Thomas Sh

'We think of Gwennap Pit, as we think of the Cathedral, as a place belonging to all of us'

Pat Griffiths
Clerk of the Preparative Meeting of Truro Religious Society of Friends and former Secretary of the Cornwall Council of Churches.

© Thomas Shaw, 1992

ISBN 0 9520163 0 3

Busveal Methodist Church Council

All rights reserved. No part of this book may be reproduced or transmitted in any form or by any means including recording or photocopying, without permission in writing from the publisher

Printed by Mid Cornwall Printing, Truro
from the authors origination.

THANKS AND ACKNOWLEDGEMENTS

I am grateful to the staff of the County Record Office and the the Local Studies Library at Redruth and particularly to Miss Angela Broome and Mr H.L. Douch of the Royal Institution of Cornwall, where most of the research behind this publication has been done, for their always willing assistance.

My thanks are due to Mr T. A . Marks for his drawing of Busveal Chapel interior as he remembered it nearly sixty years ago, and to other friends connected with Busveal who have shared reminiscences and loaned photographs.

I am grateful also to Mr Barrie S. May for reading the proofs and to Mr John Probert for sharing his discovery of John Martin's painting of 'Joshua commanding the sun to stand still' and most of all to Joan, my wife, who I know could have wished the sun to stand still while we completed a task as lengthy and demanding as Joshua's and bring this small exhausting, but not exhaustive, account of the Preaching Pit to a conclusion.

THE WESLEY TAPESTRY
1951

CONTENTS

1 THE SCARRED LANDSCAPE　　　　　　　　　　5

　　　The Mining Scene. - The first Gwennap Pit. - The Wesleys in Gwennap 1743 - 1762.

2 JOHN WESLEY'S AMPHITHEATRE 1762 - 1789　　7

　　　John Wesley at Gwennap Pit. - The Congregation - The Early Methodist Preachers. - 'My Lady's Preachers'.

3 THE PIT REMODELLED 1806-07　　　　　　　17

　　　'The King of Gwennap'. - Richard Michell and the Mine Captains - Early descriptions of the Pit - The Pit Statistics.

4 WHIT MONDAY AT THE PIT 1807 - 1976　　　23

　　　'Passing from gay to grave'. - The Missionary Platform 1818 - 1824. - Primitive Methodists, Reformers, Chartists & Others. - The Preaching Restored, 1834. - To Carharrack in the Evening. A musical People. - A Cornish Pardon Pictures and Postcards. - Sunshine and Showers. - The Pit Renovation, 1936. - The Bishop, the Congregationalist and the Politican.- Protestant Incident. - Music and Drama. - 'With the lord's permission' - Trust affairs, Caretakers and the lawn mower.

5 SPRING BANK HOLIDAY AND OTHER PIT EVENTS 1967 -　　48

　　　Finding God. - Ecumenical. - Roll Call. Summer Services.

6 BUSVEAL CHAPEL　　　　　　　　　　　　　51

　　　The blacksmith and his sons. - The early Society The 1836 Chapel. - The Sunday School.

7 PILGRIMS　　　　　　　　　　　　　　　58

　　　Panels. - The Visitor Centre. - The Chapel.- Pilgrims.

　　FOOTNOTES　　　　　　　　　　　　　　65

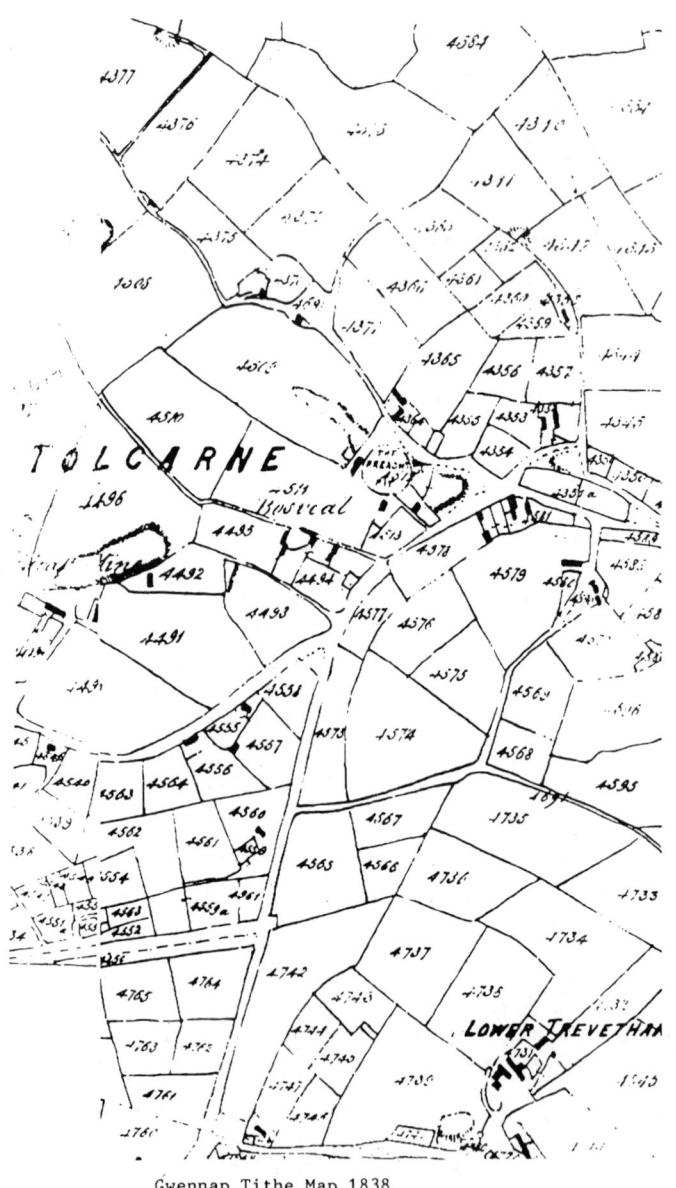

Gwennap Tithe Map 1838
showing 'The Preaching Pit'
CRO/
RIC/

1 THE SCARRED LANDSCAPE

i The Mining Scene

Visitors to Gwennap Pit sometimes express surprise because the circular hollow, resembling in size the overturned dome of St Paul's Cathedral, bears no obvious signs of the industrial use which the word 'pit' suggests, while others who have travelled in the Mediterranean, remembering the Roman open-air theatres they have seen, say that it is 'just like an amphitheatre' using the very word that John Wesley used to describe it in 1762. The industrial scene may not be evident at the Pit but it lies all around. The ivy-clad remains of the engine house at the old Chengenter Mine[1] can be seen from the rim of the Pit and the well preserved engine house at Ninnis, though not visible from the Pit, is only a quarter of a mile away, along the lane to Redruth, and many more dot the landscape, each pointing to heaven, for miles around.

Gwennap parish, with its tin and copper mines, has long been one of most populated areas in Cornwall. Beneath the surface the ground is honeycombed with mine workings, some of them so old that their exact locations must be determined by trial diggings rather than visits to the County Record Office to find documentary evidence of their existence. The workings were often at, or close to, the surface and when they collapsed from time to time, they helped to create the scarred landscape that we see today. When the foundations for the small Visitor Centre at Gwennap Pit were being dug, in 1986, a previously unknown underground tunnel thought to date back to Wesley's time, if not earlier, was discovered.[2] A writer in The Cornish Banner in 1847 said that the Pit was known to have been made by the subsidence and falling together of an old tin mine.[3]

ii The first Gwennap Pit

There have been two Gwennap Pits on the same site though not of the same dimensions or of exactly the same appearance. The old Pit was formed sometime before 1762 and was used by Wesley and others from that year until 1806. The name of the 'round field' adjoining the Pit can hardly be an indication that the Pit was an ancient plen an gwary but it may be that the Pit was commonly known as a round, and perhaps used as a cock pit long before it was used by Wesley. Because of its long association with him it is appropriate to call it 'John Wesley's Amphitheatre' as we have done in chapter two below. There are three contemporary descriptions of the old Pit.

5

Wesley described it, in 1766, as 'a round, green hollow', but qualified this by saying that it was some 200 feet across at its narrowest and 300 at its widest. It was, he said, 'a natural amphitheatre'.[4] Thomas Wills described it, in 1781, as 'circular' and said that benches had been 'cut out' in rows from top to bottom, suggesting that the terracing was, at least in part, man-made.[5] Richard Michell, in his account of the re-modelling of the Pit in 1806 said that the road (which had evidently crossed the site of the old Pit), was then re-routed to the north.[6]

The well-known lithograph of the Bradford artist, William O. Geller, showing Wesley preaching in Gwennap Pit, splendid as it is, bears no resemblance to Wesley's amphitheatre. The old Pit may have been a 'coffin' - an open trench or narrow valley, used by the tinners before Wesley's time, which bulged out at one point to form two concave half circles of banks facing each other and creating the appearance, from above, of a circle.[7] If that was the case the lane which was diverted to the north in 1806 had probably passed between the two half 'circles'. Along the slopes of this formation were the natural grassy banks on which Wesley's hearers could sit or stand, as they do in Geller's painting. There is some evidence that further benches were cut over the years to accommodate Wesley's ever growing congregations. But there was no natural rock pulpit', as Geller imagined; Wesley on his first visit 'stood on one side of this amphitheatre toward the top'.

iii The Wesleys in Gwennap

John Wesley had been a regular visitor to Gwennap for nineteen years before he discovered the Pit. The brothers Charles and John Wesley first visited the parish in 1743, Charles arriving first. A Methodist society was formed at Carharrack and a preaching room was soon built.[8] The Wesleys were not just open-air preachers. Their purpose was to revive the spiritual life of the Church of England - 'that shattered, sinking ship' as Charles Wesley described it after leaving Carharrack in 1744 - and to do this, everywhere they went they founded 'societies' for the nurture of the Christian life, the societies which were eventually to become Methodist churches.[9]

The Wesleys extended their work to Cornwall, as they did to the Midlands and the North, because it was an industrial part of the country and Methodism quickly spread among the Newcastle colliers and the Cornish tinners. An old railway poster showing a sprightly John Wesley striding across the Tamar carrying a suitcase marked 'J.W' and bearing the legend 'John Wesley was a regular visitor to Cornwall' obscured the purpose of his coming! According to tradition Charles Wesley's open air meeting on 'the green plain and the hill surrounding it' was held on the level ground in front of Carharrack Chapel. Certainly John Wesley preached standing before the front door of the preaching room in 1745. This was not the only preaching place used by the brothers: in 1746 Charles Wesley, after attending the evening service at St Euny church, Redruth, wrote 'I rode back to my own church, the valley near our room at Gwennap,'[10] and found at least five thousand sinners waiting for the glad tidings of salvation'.[11] Both the Wesleys addressed 'immense multitudes' at Gwennap in the 1740s; the sites are not known but in the later years the preaching appears to have been near Busveal for when John Wesley discovered the Pit there in 1762 he described it as being <u>close to</u> his usual preaching site. Just how close to Busveal it was we do not know.

2 JOHN WESLEY'S AMPHITHEATRE 1762-1789

i John Wesley at Gwennap Pit

Wesley's published accounts of his visits to Gwennap Pit, placed together, form an outline history of the site between 1762 and 1789: altogether he paid eighteen visits over those years[1] He was aged fifty-nine when he first used the Pit and eighty-six at his last visit. From the beginning he described the Pit as an amphitheatre.

<u>Sun. Sep. 5 1762.</u> The wind was so high at five that I could not stand in the usual place at Gwennap. But at a small distance was a hollow capable of containing many thousand people. I stood on one side of this amphitheatre toward the top, with people beneath and on all sides, and enlarged on those words from the Gospel for the day (Luke 10, 23, 24), 'Blessed are the eyes which see the things that ye see'... and hear the things which ye hear'.

<u>Sun. Sep. 8 1765</u> A still larger congregation [than the one at Redruth] was at Gwennap in the evening, equal to anything I have seen in Moorfields. Yet I think they all heard, while I enforced 'Why will ye die, O house of Israel?' [Ezekiel 18: 31 and 33: 11].

7

Sun. Sep. 14 1766. The congregation in Redruth (was) small compared with that which assembled at five in the natural amphitheatre at Gwennap, far the finest I know in the kingdom. It is a round, green hollow, gently shelving down, about fifty feet deep; but I suppose it is two hundred across one way, and near three hundred the other. I believe there were full twenty thousand people; and, the evening being calm, all could hear.

Sun. Sep. 11 1768. At five I took my old stand at Gwennap, in the natural amphitheatre. I suppose no human voice could have commanded such an audience on plain ground; but the ground rising all round gave me such an advantage that I believe all could hear distinctly.

Sun. Sep. 3 1769. I preached in the main street at Redruth...but to abundantly more at five in our amphitheatre at Gwennap; and they were so commodiously placed, row above row, that I believe all could hear.

Sun. Sep. 2 1770. At five in the evening I preached in the natural amphitheatre at Gwennap. The people covered a circle of near four score yards' diameter, and could not be fewer than twenty thousand. Yet, upon inquiry, I found they could all hear distinctly, it being a calm, still evening.

Sun. Aug. 22 1773. I preached...at five in the amphitheatre at Gwennap. The people both filled it, and covered the ground round about to a considerable distance. So that, supposing the space to be four score-yards square, and to contain five persons in a square yard, there must be above two-and-thirty thousand people; the largest assembly I ever preached to. Yet I found, upon inquiry, all could hear, even to the skirts of the congregation! Perhaps the first time that a man of seventy had been heard by thirty-thousand persons at once!

Sun. Sep. 4 1774 ...the glorious congregation assembled at five, in the amphitheatre at Gwennap. They were judged to cover four-score yards, and yet those farthest off could hear.

Sun. Sep. 3 1775. At five in the evening [I preached] in the amphitheatre at Gwennap. I think this is the most magnificent spectacle which is to be seen on this side of heaven. And no music is to be heard upon earth comparable to the sound of many thousand voices, when they are all harmoniously joined together singing praises to God and the Lamb.

Sun. Aug. 25 1776. About five in the evening I began preaching at Gwennap, to full twenty thousand persons. And they were so commodiously placed, in the calm, still evening, that every one heard distinctly.

Sun. Aug. 31 1777. I preached...in the evening to the hugh congregation at Gwennap, larger (it was supposed) by fifteen hundred or two thousand than ever it had been before.

Sun. Aug. 30 1778. About five I preached in the amphitheatre at Gwennap, it was believed, to four-and-twenty thousand. Afterwards I spent a solemn hour with the society, and slept in peace.

Sun. Aug. 27 1780. It was supposed twenty thousand people were assembled at the amphitheatre in Gwennap. And yet all, I was informed, could hear distinctly, in the fair, calm evening.

Sun. Sep. 2 1781. About five in the evening I preached at Gwennap, I believe two or three and twenty thousand were present, and I believe God enabled me so to speak that even those who stood farthest off could hear distinctly. I think this is my ne plus ultra. I shall scarce see a larger congregation till we meet in the air.

Sun. Sep. 1 1782. Afterwards I expounded the Parable of the Sower at Gwennap, to how many thousands I know not. But all (I was informed) could hear distinctly. 'This is the Lord's doing'.

On three of Wesley's visits to the Pit, 1762, 1765 and 1785, he he gives the texts from which he preached. The Methodist circuit preaching plan had a small beginning in Wesley's time but he himself made his own plan and, with the Cornish societies in mind he made sure that he was at Gwennap Pit at 5 p.m. on one Sunday during each visit.

In his sixties, after a serious fall from his horse on London Bridge, Wesley very reluctantly took his friends' advice and began to use a post chaise on his longer journeys and one of them gave him a two horse chaise in 1766. These new arrangements didn't prevent him from hiring or borrowing a horse when necessary, as he did to cross the sands near Perranporth on one occasion, and to make an urgent visit to St Gennys from Camelford on another. His expenses along the road were met by the circuits through which he passed. So we find in the West Cornwall (later the Redruth) Circuit account book[2] such items as:

1776	Pd for Turnpicks (sic) Hostlers when Mr Wesley was with us		10	6
1777	paid for oats for Mr Wesley's horses		5	0
1780	To washing Mr Wesley's linnen		1	9½
1782	To 10 days for a chaise for Mr Wesley	£6	5	0
	To the driver 10 days		15	0
	For keeping Mr Wesley's horses	£2	17	5
	Pd for postage of a letter for Mr Wesley & given to the driver		7	6
1785	Horses and driver with Mr Wesley	£5	0	6
	Mr Wesley toward expenses	£3	6	1½
1789	To expense on account of Mr Wesley ...		4 7	2
	To pd for Mr Wesley's Horses		1 2	5

A payment of 6s 2½d to Richard Williams of Carharrack in 1789 may have had something to do with Wesley's last visit. Williams, who received three letters from Wesley may well have been his host when he visited Gwennap Pit in the later years.

Wesley's surviving diaries (from which he later wrote up the Journal), complete the picture of the last three of his visits to the Pit, and show the old man resolutely following the endless round of engagements which had begun more than forty years before.

In 1785, after sleeping overnight at Redruth, he rose at 4, his usual time, said his prayers, wrote a few letters , drank a cup of tea and rode in the hired chaise to St Agnes for a service at 8.30 a.m. Returning to Redruth he found time for more letter writing before dinner at 12.30. He preached again at 1.30,

10

and then returned to his correspondence for the third time that day. Then, after attending evening prayer at St Euny church[3] and taking tea, he left in the chaise for Gwennap Pit at 4.15. He later wrote in his Journal:

> Sun. Aug. 28 1785. I was afraid lest I should not be able to make all those hear that assembled [at Gwennap Pit] in the evening. But though it was supposed there were two or three thousand more than ever there were before, yet they heard (I was afterwards informed) to the very skirts of the congregation, while I applied those solemn words, 'One thing is needful'.[Luke 10: 42].

After the service he met the members of the Methodist society (possibly at Busveal but probably at Carharrack),[4] visited a few people, had supper at 8 o'clock and went to bed at 9.30. He was 82.

Two years later, on another Sunday, and following a similar programme, he preached and gave communion at Hayle, and preached again at Redruth before reaching Gwennap Pit for the 5 p.m. service. In the Pit he preached from Isaiah 66, and later wrote:

> Sun. Sep. 9 1787. About five I began in the pit at Gwennap. I suppose we had a thousand more than ever were there before. But it was all one; my voice was strengthened accordingly, so that every one could hear distinctly.

After the service he conducted a lovefeast: it would have been held at Carharrack, Busveal, or Redruth. He was 84.

At the time of Wesley's last visit to the Pit (and also to Cornwall) in 1789, now aged 86, he was still following the exacting daily routine that he had kept up for more than forty years. Rising at 4 a.m. at his hosts' in Redruth he dressed and said his prayers and then (unusually) fell asleep again, but by 5.45 he was writing a narrative for publication. At 10.30 he attended morning service at St Euny church, and afterwards called on some of his friends before dinner. After dinner he slept awhile and woke again for prayers and reading. At 5 p.m., he was at Gwennap Pit where he preached his last sermon there, on the healing of Naaman (II Kings 5: 14). He wrote in his Journal:

> Sun. Aug. 23 1789. I preached...in the evening at the amphitheatre, I suppose, for the last time; for my voice cannot now command the still increasing multitude. It

11

> was supposed they were now more than five-and-twenty thousand. I think it scarce possible that all should hear.

That last day concluded with a society meeting, conversation and prayers, before he went to bed at 9.30.

The subject of all Wesley's sermons was Jesus Christ the Saviour of all who will come to him. One of his pregnant phrases was "I offered Christ" and for that reason the first line on the first panel at the entrance to the Pit today was placed there to summarize his message to all who pass by:

> O let me commend my Saviour to you,
> I set to my seal that Jesus is true.

That is the raison d'etre of Gwennap Pit. Everything in Wesley's theology and social teaching related to this central, pivotal theme. 'I think it meet, right and my bounden duty' he wrote, echoing the phrase from the prayer book,'to declare unto all who are willing to hear, the glad tidings of salvation'. There were many who dated their conversion from the day they heard him preach at Gwennap Pit and, as at least one onlooker on the wider Cornish scene saw it, 'he taught the vulgar to be sober, honest and industrious and to deal fairly with each other'.[5]

ii   The Congregation

Wesley's hearers at the Pit were, of course, as mixed a company of people as can be found at any open air gathering. Many of them were members of the societies which he or his helpers had established in the mining communities but even they were people with different degrees of commitment to the Methodist way of life, there were saints among them such as Elizabeth Harpur of Redruth who Wesley thought was an example to be commended.[6] There were also backsliders and, in Methodist parlance, 'backsliders recovered' like the one who sent Wesley a note (handed to him at the Pit?) signed 'A vile backslider from the pure love of Jesus, and from the society at Gwennap'.[7] And there were also those in an uncertain category, like Grace Paddy - 'a well-bred sensible young woman', as she appeared to Wesley, who attended the innermost circle of membership at Redruth and yet who 'wore a large glittering necklace' quite contrary to the rule book.[8] Few of them can be named at this distance of time, Richard Williams, the steward at Carharrack, who wrote to John Wesley about numbers in the Pit and about American slavery was certainly one of them,[9] and so was the eleven year old James Thomas who walked six miles from his home at Bolenowe to hear Wesley on his last visit to the Pit.[10]
And in serried ranks of the great congregation there must have been, from the very beginning, those who just came 'for the fun of the thing'.[11]

It is impossible to estimate the number of Wesley's hearers at the Pit, whether 20,000 (in 1766), 32,000 (in 1773), or 'more than 25,000' at his last visit. These figures were probably submitted to Wesley at his request, after the services, and he usually accepted them. Replying to a letter from Richard Williams after his visit in 1774 Wesley wrote, '...Fifty yards square (allowing five to a yard which is the lowest computation) will contain twelve thousand five hundred persons. But here they stood far beyond the edge of the Pit on all sides'.[12]

Such estimates, of course, were not realistic. Although Wesley noted that the congregation sometimes overflowed the boundary of the Pit, 34,000, his highest estimate, would be impossible, but we can certainly think in terms of thousands. The congregation in 1802 was estimated by the preacher, without any suggestion of it being an unusually low turnout, as around 1,200 at the most.[13]

Most of the people present would have come from the mining communities in mid and west Cornwall and in vast numbers from around Gwennap and Redruth. Many villages would have been denuded of half their inhabitants on the days when it was known that Mr Wesley would be at the Pit. As Foolish Dick of Porthtowan recalled many years later, 'When Maaster Wesley was at the Pit..aall the neighburs were flockin' away to hear 'un'.[14]

Apart from the inflated estimates of the numbers in the Pit congregation the wonder is that Wesley, especially in his later years, could have been heard as well as he was. In his sixties he was wondering whether they could all hear him, and in his seventies he was claiming confidently not only that all could hear but that all could hear distinctly. His last word, however, at the age of eighty-six was 'I think it scarce possible that all should hear'. By that time of course people were going to the pit as much to see the venerable man as with the hope of hearing him.

It has often been said that 'Methodism was born in song' but, if that was the case, it was not any in kind of song but in the hymns of Charles Wesley. From the very beginning the Pit must have resounded with the full throated strains of praise.

>   O for a thousand tongues to sing
>   My great Redeemer's praise!
>   The glories of my God and King,
>   The triumphs of his grace!

If Wesley visited Gwennap Pit today he would hear the same Scriptures read, though not often in the version with which he was familiar, and hear some of the same hymns sung, though most of the tunes, even those thought of today as 'the old Methodist tunes' would be unfamiliar to him: they came after his time.

Where did John Wesley stand when he preached at the Pit? Below the rim of the Pit he tells us, and the siting of the two granite posts in the present Pit, placed there in 1807, may be an indication that he usually selected that area.

Wesley today would rejoice that the preaching tradition he had begun was still continuing. He would look less approvingly at the long-handled collection boxes for, antique as they may be today, his Methodist members were expected to give regularly and generously but not to take a collection in a service. Wesley would be intrigued by the amplifier; he was always interested in new inventions and willing to use them in the service of God.

iii The Early Methodist Preachers

Wesley created an order of travelling preachers whom he sent around the country as his representatives though they were normally 'stationed' in one circuit for twelve months or longer, and after his death in 1791 the Conference inherited his authority to appoint them. The travelling preachers, especially those stationed in Cornwall, used the Pit from time to time, and others, such as Joseph Benson in 1795 and Thomas Taylor in 1799, came to Gwennap in the course of specially arranged tours of Cornwall.

Benson's visit was long remembered. On Sunday, 21 June 1795 he preached at St Agnes in the morning and then hastened to Gwennap where he preached 'in the celebrated "PIT" where he was provided with a table for a platform which gave him a full view of his congregation which was estimated at about twenty thousand persons'.[15] Anna Reynalds of Truro was present and heard him preach from Revelation xx 11f: 'Then I saw a great white throne...and I saw the dead, great and small, standing before the throne, and the books were opened. And also another book was opened, which is the book of life'.[16]

Elizabeth Flamank of St Austell who had known Wesley since she was a small child was also there.[17] Forty years later there were Cornish Methodists who still spoke 'with rapture and astonishment of the marvellous ingenuity, appropriateness and power' of Benson's sermon.[18] A 'very old Methodist' had a clear remembrance of that service seventy-six years later. It seems that even John Wesley was equalled or outdone that day!

Thomas Taylor was at the Pit on Sunday, 25 May 1799 for what was evidently the annual service. He was told that it had been advertised for twenty miles around. 'It was amazing' he thought 'to see horse and foot flocking from all parts, and some carriages' - there must have been hundreds of horses, and a multitude of poor little ragged boys who had come to earn a penny by holding the horses a proper distance from the congregation. Only once before had he preached to so large a congregation and that was on the Green at Glasgow.[19]

Richard Treffry, the superintendent of the Truro circuit, in which Gwennap at that time was included, came to the Pit on Sunday October 10th 1802 with a Mr Nile of Bristol who had a brief to collect for the reduction of a debt on the chapel there. He preached to about 1,000 people in the Pit on Ezekiel 18: 30b,'Repent, and turn from all your transgressions so iniquity shall not be your ruin'.[20]

iv 'My Lady's Preachers'

Wesley's societies in the early days were part of a wider movement of 'religious societies' which could be described as Methodist in the widest sense of the word. There was a theological division between those who were Arminians, the followers of Wesley, who believed that God's grace was for 'all mankind' and the Calvinists (the followers of George Whitefield) who held that salvation was only for the elect. Wesley and Whitefield, both Anglican priests, despite their deep differences, maintained their friendship throughout but there was always friction, in Cornwall and elsewhere, between the two parts of 'Methodism'. In the end, Calvinistic Methodism became virtually confined to Wales, although in Cornwall it became established in a few places, largely through the encouragement of a lady of Calvinistic views, the Countess of Huntingdon, who had built up a group of societies into a little Methodism of her own - 'Lady Huntingdon's Connexion'. She built a training college for her ministers at Trevecca in South Wales.

Thomas Wills, an evangelical curate of St Agnes, who left the Church of England to become one of 'My Lady's Preachers' preached at the Pit twice (between two of Wesley's visits) in 1781 and left the only contemporary description of the old Pit that we have other than Wesley's.[21] It is interesting to place Wills' description of his services alongside those provided by Wesley: there are many similarities. He writes,

> [Sunday, July 1 1781] In the afternoon, I went to Bosveal, and at five o'clock, ... found many thousands assembled in a large, deep hollow ground, which is rendered convenient for the preacher, and an innumerable multitude of hearers, by circular benches cut out of the pit, in rows from top to bottom. I am at a loss to form any computation of the number; but they were supposed to be not less than ten thousand. The word was received with the utmost solemnity. The text was Isa. 27 last verse, Indeed the sound of the great trumpet seemed to reach the hearts of many; and the call to the outcasts, and those that were ready to perish, was heard with great brokenness of heart and tears...The word, I trust, ran with power; and the Lord, of a truth graced this assembly with his presence.

Sunday, July 22. In the afternoon, we went to Bosveal, and found a large multitude assembled from almost all the towns, and most of the the principal parishes within thirty miles of the western part of Cornwall, where I had preached during the tour. It was the largest congregation I ever beheld, and judged by everyone to be above ten thousand. An universal solemnity and awe sat on every countenance, and the Lord was in the midst of us. Even the people of the world were reminded of the judgment-day, from beholding this innumerable and deeply-affected multitude. Gospel preachers[22] with their congregations, from many miles round, attended on this occasion. The subject was taken from Matt. xi 4,5. 'Go and shew John again these things which ye do hear and see;...the blind receive their sight, the lame walk, the lepers are cleansed, the deaf hear, the dead are raised up, and the poor have the gospel preached unto them'.

Though I had a great cold and hoarseness some part of the day, my voice was clear throughout the whole sermon; and I was heard distinctly by the most distant people that filled and surrounded this pit, near Lady Huntingdon's chapel.[23] All were still, notwithstanding the immense number assembled, throughout the whole service, as if there had been but ten persons present, and the people say there had never been such a large company assembled there on any former occasion.[24]

An old man, in the name of many others, earnestly intreated that they might have more constant and frequent preaching in Gwenap, from the students, than has hitherto been; and I promised they should be more constantly attended to.[25]

The ageing Rowland Hill, another Anglican Calvinist minister, who also worked with the Countess for a time, and had been one of Wesley's critics, came to the remodelled Pit in 1819, - but more of him later.

3 THE PIT REMODELLED 1806-7

i 'The King of Gwennap'

Over the period of Wesley's visits and the remodelling of the site the amphitheatre was a tenement in the Manor of Tolcarne in the possession of the Duke of Buckingham and other absentee landlords and they or their tenants were willing to allow the Methodist preachers whether Wesleyan or Calvinistic to use the Pit presumably free of charge.

At this period the Williams family of Scorrier House were establishing themselves as mine adventurers and landowners and were eventually to purchase the Manor of Tolcarne as well as other lands in the parish and elsewhere. John Williams (1753-1841) was a successful mining adventurer. A mine owner, landowner and founder of a county family, he was at the same time a man with the common touch. He was known to everyone in the parish as 'The King of Gwennap'. It was an appropriate title for he had an economic hold over almost every family in the parish. He became a Methodist and worshipped at Wheal Rose chapel which he is said to have built himself; a Church-Methodist, himself he had ecumenical connections if not also sympathies. When he was asked by a lawyer to what denomination he belonged he said 'I am a Methodist'. He was then asked about his sons - 'What is John?' - he is a Quaker; 'What is Michael?' - he is a Churchman. 'Make William a Jew' said the lawyer 'and you will be a match for the devil.'[1]

John Williams gave financial support and perhaps used his influence with the landlords to get their permission for the Pit to be remodelled as a memorial to John Wesley. He presided at a missionary meeting in the Pit in 1826.[2] and was probably the first of the family to occupy a 'squire's pew' at the annual service.

ii Richard Michell and the Mine Captains

Gwennap Pit as we see it today is the work of an impressive band of tinners and their helpers who, during the winter of 1806-07, cleared the site of the old Pit, re-directed the lane which once crossed it, and made a geometrically designed amphitheatre surrounded by a high wall. At that period, and later, there were many young children employed at the surface of the mines and as late as 1871 there were a number of men, in their 'seventies, living in the district, who well remembered carrying small stones in their pinafores to help in the building of the Pit.[3]

The work was planned by four mine captains (mine managers), John Martin, John Dennis, William Davey and Thomas Trestrail and a mine engineer, Richard Michell, who if not the originator of the scheme, seems to have played a leading part in it. A preliminary meeting was held at Busveal, perhaps in the house

17

of William Davey of North Busveal, and plans prepared for the reconstruction of the Pit as a memorial to John Wesley.[4] Whether the scheme was launched on their own initiative or, more probably, on behalf of the Redruth circuit, is not known. An appeal was launched and £71 raised, towards which the Redruth Methodists contributed £6 and the Tuckingmill society £5 18 0.

The work, of course, had the full support of John Williams who was the 'principal subscriber' to the scheme. Probably, like Williams, the four 'captains' were also members of the Methodist society: Thomas Trestrail was the society steward at Kerley.

More is known about Richard Michell (1748-1836), the steam engineer. His father, Thomas Michell of Bell (in Lanner), who was later a mine captain at Polgooth near St Austell, is said to have been 'an early convert of John Wesley'. Richard, himself, according to family tradition, held Wesley in high regard, (which does not necessarily mean that he was a member of the Methodist society). He erected steam engines in the local mines for Boulton and Watt. His great-great-grandson quotes him as saying "no two men have been of so much use or have done so much good for the County as the Revd Mr John Wesley with respect to religion and Mr James Watt with his automatical machines. Mr Wesley sought out and taught the vulgar to be sober, honest, and industrious, to deal fairly with each other...he not only taught them to live well but to die well...Mr Watt taught them to be industrious and help'd them to get at the vast treasure which providence till then had hid in the bowells of their country".[5] A bound copy of the Methodist Magazine, 1804 at the RIC which belonged to Richard Sampson of Carharrack in 1820 is inscribed 'Captn Richd Michell departed this life November 6th 1828, and entered [into rest] Sunday 9th inst whose name is ever dear to me. Richd Sampson'

The work began on 19 November 1806. The old site was cleared, the existing open shafts leading to ancient workings were capped, and the lane from Carnmarth was turned to the north of the Pit. A bank of earth was piled up in a great circle and a nine foot high wall (360' in circumference) built to enclose it. The wall and the bank were opened in two places, one on either side of the Pit, to form entrances into the new (and possibly more limited) area within it.

An iron gate was placed at each entrance. On the inner face of the encircling bank concentric terraces of grass covered seats were arranged, as we see them today, reminiscent of the natural terraces of the old Pit. John Wesley would still have recognised his amphitheatre.

iii Early descriptions of the Pit

When the Pit had been re-modelled and the opening service had been held, on Whit Monday 1807, Richard Michell sat down to write an account of the work that had been done; he wrote:[6]

> In the year 1806 Nov 19 Cap Jn⁰ Martin Cap Jn⁰ Dawe Cap W Davey Cap Th⁰ Trestrail and myself meet at Busveal and agreed to repair the —————————— Pit in respect to and in memory of Mr Wesley we had liberty of the Lords steward Mr Wm Jenkin[s] Mr Jn⁰ Mosser to do as we thought fit by this spot of land (where the old Pit stood) for the purpose of a place for the Methodists to preach in — men were set to work — the shafts were filled up the road turned to the north of it
>
> It was finished and had preaching in it on the 18 of June 1807. the whole repairs amounted to £71·14·4 the greatest part of which was raised by subscription — the remainder by Collection. The Principal subscribers were
> Jn⁰ Willer Esqre Jn⁰ Messe Esq
> Mr W Roberts Cap W Davy   the Pitt is 360 feet
> J Trestral J Dawe Capt Jn⁰ mater or 114 feet in diamet.
> Mr Michell &c &c [Steam Engineer]   and contains 10,200 □
> at the first preaching was collected   feet
> 14 pound &c &c —
>   It is 16 feet diameter at Bottom and 360 feet in Circum. or 114 feet diameter at top by 20 feet deep / side 9 feet high/
>   gate 20 feet mason work by 6 feet high
>
> Wesley's Pitt began to be repaired on the 19 of November 1806 and on Whit Monday 18 June 1807 there was preach^g in it at which time there was collected towards the work 14 pounds The total was 71·14·4

'Redruth society gave toward it 6 pounds
Tuckingmill society gave £ 5 " 18 . —
The persons who laid the plan and begunit were
— Capt Jn Martin   ⎫ directed the work
  Cap Jn Dennis   ⎬ and laid the plan
  Cap.t W.m Davey   ⎪ ~~and laid the plan~~
  Cap Tho Trestrail ⎪ [the] helpers [were the
  Rich.d Michell   ⎭ neighbouring minersthe
  [Steam Engineer]

Richard Michell's account and the sketch plan of the Pit have both been preserved by his descendants and may originally have belonged together [7] In the drawing the Pit is viewed from the splatt at the North Busveal entrance at the point where the road had once turned on to the Pit site.

The Trevena engraving,[8] which can perhaps be dated to the 1840s, if the name 'Albert' on the van by the gate is any guide, shows the two granite posts in situ with a preacher standing between them, but there is no post laid across the top as described by Entwisle. - see below.

Gwennap Pit, Cornwall

"I think this is the most magnificent spectacle which is to be seen on this side Heaven"
John Wesley 1775

Michell's account of the reconstruction of the Pit can be supplemented from two other sources, both dated 1827. Richard Thomas of Falmouth, a land surveyor and civil engineer, writing in that year, described the Pit as having been 'formed by a mound of earth containing within it an inverted conical hollow' which has round it 'a rough circular wall, as high as the bank, and two entrance gates with steps on opposite parts of the circumference...' 'The interior' he says, is made like an amphitheatre with turf seats extending quite round: its diameter is about 125 feet, and the depth of the centre is about 20 feet below the circumference.[9]

The other description, of the same date, was made by Joseph Entwisle who was heading a missionary deputation to Cornwall in

February that year. He was staying at Carharrack with Captain Joe Mitchell, and from there he wrote to his wife,

'I walked a mile to see the celebrated pit at Gwennap where Mr Wesley preached. It is circular, enclosed by a high wall, and has two entrances by gates, which are kept locked. The miners have made it most complete. There are rows upon rows of seats in a circular form from top to bottom. These seats are parted with stones to keep them in form, and are covered with a green carpet; for now the grass is quite green, and the surface as level and regular as possible. On one side, a few yards below the top of the pit, is a pulpit; that is, two large stones standing upright, with one across, to lay the books on. This amphitheatre is regarded by the lord of the manor as in the possession of the Methodists, and for their exclusive use.'[10]

It was probably because Entwisle was at the Pit on a February morning that his description included the granite blocks and the green carpet in winter, so evident in the empty Pit. Visitors who only see the Pit when it is full are not aware of the stones but only of a mass of people. Joseph Wood from the St Austell Circuit, who preached there in 1834, recorded that 'This vast amphitheatre was crowded, presenting one unbroken cloud of human beings from the bottom to the utmost verge of the enclosure.'[11]

iv The Pit Statistics

Visitors often ask how many people the Pit will contain. Assessments have ranged widely, from 1.000 to 10,000!. The highest estimates, wildly inaccurate, were made in the early nineteenth century, those toward the end of the century were more modest, generally around 2-3,000. The numbers attending showed no sign of lessening after the death of Wesley, but estimates of the size of the congregation in the new Pit were usually as inflated as they had been in the old Pit. It was said there were 10,000 in 1808, 'an immense concourse' and 'a great number who could not possibly find room in the Pit' in 1827, thousands' with 'hundreds outside' in 1834 and seven to ten thousand in 1838. In that year however the Falmouth Express reporter made a more realistic assessment, 'We doubt' he wrote, 'if more than 5,000 ever were, or could be assembled in it. This calculation is easily made. Being a circle of 120 feet diameter, it includes a surface of 11,309 square feet. Allowing to each individual 18 inches square it would contain rather more than 5,000; but this would be packing them like fish in a cask. Besides, the front rank in each circle is seated and therefore each occupies the standing room of two persons'[12]

In 1966 Mr R.R. Blewett, the schoolmaster at St Day at that time, made an estimate based on very careful measurements in which he involved some of the older children. He presented the results at a meeting of the Federation of Old Cornwall

Societies held at the Pit, and this was later published in his serialised papers, These Things Have Been. According to his report, the diameter of the Pit, (measured across the inner circumference of the top circle) is 109'; all the thirteen rings, except the bottom three are 4' wide; and, (measured along the circumference of the circle), range from 342' down to 53'. The total length of the thirteen circumferences (including the two gangways) is 2,514' and this (allowing 18" per person) would provide seats for 1,676 people. 200 more could stand (as they often did) on the top shelf and a further 100 could squat (as they often did) between the rows and on the small area at the bottom, thus increasing the total congregation to 1,976. Of course, if the congregation all stood along the terraces (five to a square yard) the total would swell to 5,675, but, as Mr Blewett humorously concluded, 'If such a thing were attempted it would result in an audience of nil the following year'[13].

4 WHIT MONDAY AT THE PIT
1807 - 1966

i Passing from gay to grave

The opening of the re-modelled Pit in 1807 was not reported in the recently established Royal Cornwall Gazette; all we know about the service was that a collection for the reconstruction fund raised £14![1] In the following year, however, the Gazette reported under the heading 'The Holidays','The several fairs...lost nothing of their wonted attraction; never were they more fully attended - but passing from gay to grave let us close with the assemblage of persons who attended on Monday at the Pit, in Gwennap, where three Methodist preachers zealously attempted to persuade nearly ten thousand persons to renounce 'the pomps and vanities of this wicked world'.[2] The 'grave' element at the Pit, in contrast to the 'gaiety' of the holiday fairs, was again noted in 1809 when it was stated that the day was spent in prayer and exhortation'.[3]

A comment on the nature of Methodist gravity appeared in the Gazette in 1814 in which it was stated that 'Whatever opinion may be entertained [about the Methodists'] peculiar doctrinal sentiments and of the appearances sometimes exhibited in their Meetings, all must feel gratified in contemplating the moral effects produced by their preaching on the lower orders of society...where drunkenness has given place to sobriety, and bacchanalian conflicts to peace and harmony'.[4]

The preachers of this period are seldom named and never quoted, but we know that Richard Treffry of Penzance (a future President of the Conference) and William Martin of Helston were among the preachers at the Pit on Whit Monday, 1814.[5]

23

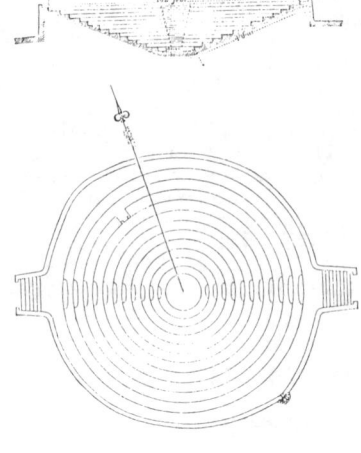

'Christian Miscellany', 1868

Plan of Gwennap Pit

Aerial View of Gwennap Pit, 1991 - Sky Library (Kettering)

24

The crowds thronged to the Pit from towns, villages and hamlets within a ten or twenty-mile radius. Many of them arrived, like Foolish Dick's 'neighburs', on foot, on horseback, by gig, or horse and trap. Local vans (primitive horse-drawn buses) were also available from nearby towns, like the 'Albert' shown in Trevena's lithograph.

ii The Missionary Platform

With the blessing of John Wesley and the advocacy of Thomas Coke (see the panels in the Visitor Centre at the Pit) Methodists from the early days saw Overseas Missions as a practical extension of their evangelical work, and from around 1813 there was a surge of interest in the World parish among Methodists as there was also in the Church of England and among the nonconformists. This missionary zeal was reflected at Gwennap Pit in 1817 when a collection was taken at the service for overseas missions.[6]

In 1821 it was announced that the meeting usually held in the Pit would be held instead in the Methodist chapel in the parish (evidently Carharrack) and that 'instead of sermons which have been usually preached, appeal will be urged, and a collection made in behalf of the very numerous and successful missions which have been established by the Methodists in various parts of the world'.[7]

In 1823, this time on account of unfavourable weather, the Pit service was again held at Carharrack. Dr Robert Newton, who was to be four times President of the Conference, and was one of the foremost missionary advocates in Methodism, was leading a missionary deputation to Cornwall and was on the platform that Whit Monday. He is not named in the local press report, which gave its space to two of the other speakers, the Rev John Waterhouse, a future missionary in the South Seas, who told the congregation that there were 600 millions of people without the Gospel, and only 400 missionaries to preach to them, and Titus Close, a missionary from Madras who spoke about heathen superstitions, and 'appeared to rivet the attention of his hearers'. It was announced that the Gwennap friends had been active in procuring aid from their neighbours; one labouring miner in Gwennap had contributed £5 to the fund.[8]

In 1825 the Rev Walter Lawry, a Wesleyan minister and a native of Gorran, spoke about his work in the Friendly Islands, as did other missionaries from other (unspecified) denominations. They spoke from a platform specially erected in the Pit.[9] In the following year the chair was taken by John Williams of Scorrier House.

In 1819 Rowland Hill, an Anglican Calvinist minister who, like Thomas Wills, had worked with the Countess of Huntingdon for a time, preached a missionary sermon at the Pit. A histrionic figure, Hill was ready made for the satirical pen of

Richard Polwhele, the vicar of Kenwyn and critic of Methodism. Polwhele wrote, on 30 August 1819: 'Rowland Hill that hoary itinerant (now 75) is at this moment entertaining some of my parishioners at the Pitt...in Gwennap with his Otaheitan stories, clapping horns upon his idols, and exhibiting gods turned devils to the admiration of a gaping multitude!'[10]

In 1834 the 'preaching service' was restored but the missionary collection continued, and was still being taken in 1911. The long-handled collecting boxes of uncertain age which were in use in 1931, and are still used at Pit services today, may well have been made for these missionary occasions.

In 1843 a collection was taken at the Pit for the relief of mission chapels in the West Indies which had been 'injured by the late earthquake'.[11] A century later, in 1940, the Rev Harold Rattenbury addressed a gathering in the Pit on his return from visiting China and Burma,[12] Another fifty years on, in 1990, a set of panels (prepared by the Mission House) was placed in the newly opened Visitor Centre to illustrate the worldwide spread of Wesley's world parish and provide a window on world mission today.

iii Primitive Methodists, Reformers, Chartists and others

In 1827 a visitor to the Pit reported that it was 'regarded by the lord of the manor as in the possession of the Methodists, and for their exclusive use.'[13] By 'Methodists' he meant the Wesleyans and it would seem from this that other groups who wished to hold events there had to obtain permission from them even before the Wesleyans themselves had any legal title to the site.

After Wesley's death Methodism became fragmented, and around 1830 the Primitive Methodists from the north of England formed a base for their mission at Redruth and held two Camp-Meetings (open-air gatherings) in the Pit, it would seem with Wesleyan approval. In 1832 Hugh Bourne, one of their founders, paid a visit to the Pit though he didn't preach there. He saw the grassy circles, 'seat above seat' forming 'a large circular gallery'. The Wesleyan Methodists, he said, usually had preaching in it about once a year, and added, 'Our people have held two powerful Camp Meetings in it'.[14] The surprising thing is that the Westcountry Bible Christians, also open-air preachers, do not appear to have used the Pit - at least there is no record that they did.

The greatest division in Wesleyan Methodism occured in 1849 following the expulsion of three ministers who had led the reform movement in Methodism, Everett, Griffiths and Dunn. Samuel Dunn was a Mevagissey man and later the superintendent of the Camborne circuit. At the time of the expulsions he made a tour of Cornwall, and at St Columb he laid down a challenge to the leading Wesleyans in Cornwall to meet him in public debate 'on Goss Moor or in Gwennap Pit'.[15] Neither meeting was held. Thomas Garland of Illogan pointed out that 'the Pit is not public property; and the gentleman who has charge of it, thinking its historical reputation would be tarnished by such a discussion as Mr Dunn proposes would not consent to have it there.'[16]

'The gentleman in charge' was evidently the superintendent minister, one of whose predecessors, ten years earlier, had refused the Chartists permission to use the Pit for a political gathering. The Chartists, the militant tendency of the time, demanded no more than the enfranchisement which came later, but they were suspect on every hand 'misguided men' as the Whig West Briton called them, and 'mischievious people' as the Tory Gazette called them. Although their founder, William Lovett, was a Cornishman, they found less support among the Cornish miners than they had hoped for.

They had hoped to have had the use of the Pit for a mass rally on Easter Monday 1839, but despite the statement of the Redruth diarist Thomas Nicoll on that date that 'the Chartists held a meeting to Day at the Pit', the press report of the meeting in the Pit, and the later publication of the 'Address of the Radical Reformers of the Western Division of... Cornwall in Public Meeting assembled at Gwennap Pitt to the General Convention of the Industrus Classes, dated Gwennap Pitt April 1st 1839, there seems clear evidence that the meeting was not held in the Pit.[17]

The Royal Cornwall Gazette reported:

> It will scarcely be credited that these fellows had the assurance to advertise their meeting to be held in THE PIT at Gwennap, a place - as most of our readers know - consecrated by the ministrations of the venerable founder of Methodism, and still retained by his followers for periodical religious worship. The Methodists knew better what was due to their own character, and to the memory of Wesley, than to suffer this profanation; the senior minister of the circuit very properly repaired to the spot with the parish constables, and kept the gates against all intrusion.[18]

The 'senior minister', the superintendent of the Gwennap Circuit, later received a letter from the vicar of Gwennap complimenting him on his action. The element of uncertainty remains but the probability is that the Chartists were refused the use of the Pit but held an open air gathering somewhere in its vicinity, hence the conflicting reports.

The first use of the Pit by a non-religious organisation seems to have been a teetotal gathering in 1839. The Teetotal Movement was brought to Cornwall by James Teare in 1838 and resulted in the formation of Teetotal societies in many places including Redruth and Gwennap. The Teetotal movement did not have the official approval of the Wesleyan Conference, but this evidently did not prevent the them from using the Pit in 1839, ten weeks after it had been closed to the Chartists. There was a joint procession of the two local societies from Redruth to the Pit where the gathering was addressed by 'Messrs Richards, Parsons, Curtis and Boot'.[19] By 1886 an annual Sunday afternoon service of the United Friendly Societies had become established and it was reported in that year to have included Oddfellows, Foresters, Philanthropies and Rechabites who had marched in procession from Redruth to the Pit led by the Volunteer and Town Mission bands. A service was then conducted by 'various ministers of the town' and a collection taken for the Miners' Hospital.[20]

iv The Preaching Restored

In 1834 the 'preaching service' was restored in place of the missionary meeting, the preacher that year being Joseph Wood the superintendent of the Camborne circuit. According to the Gazette he 'delivered an impressive sermon' but his own account is more informative: he writes -

> 'This vast amphitheatre was crowded, presenting one unbroken cloud of human beings from the bottom to the utmost verge of the enclosure, and by some who were there I was informed that there were many hundreds outside who could not gain admittance. Considering that the voice ascends, I stood lower on one side of the pit than the preachers generally have been accustomed to do. I also stood so as to have the the wind at my back, which was a help in carrying forward my voice, and those who stood farthest off on the opposite side said they could distinctly hear while I published 'the grace of God bringeth salvation unto all men', etc. The sight of such a concourse is awfullly impressive; and, while standing among the collected thousands, the whole of whom rising on the terraced interior of the Pit are visible, one is powerfully impressed with a sense of one's own individual insignificance. Having put forth all my strength in order to be heard, I felt somewhat exhausted...[21]

The preachers at the Pit between 1834 and 1932 were, like Joseph Wood, mostly ministers from Cornish circuits who were known for their eloquence or other abilities. One exception was in 1862 when the Rev John Rattenbury concluded his presidency at the Camborne Conference and came over to preach at the Pit though that, of course, was not the annual

service.[22]   The congregations listened to Mr Wood's 'impressive sermon' in 1834, and to Mr Kellatt's 'admirable sermon' in 1864.[23] A 'sermon of average quality' by Mr Andrew was noted in 1876,[24] but Mr Back's sermon, in 1888,was evidently above the average because the same observer says of him that 'he is beyond controversy the most able Methodist minister in Cornwall at the present time'.[25] These assessments came from the pen of 'Quizzy' the candid correspondent to the <u>Royal Cornwall Gazette</u> in the 1870s, whose observations have been useful in the compilation of
this record. In 1884 he suggested that 'Many ministers who labour in Cornwall have an eye on the Pit, where they may display their sacred oratory on the spot where John Wesley stood....but it is reserved for only a few. Mental vigour, apart from physical strength, does not qualify a man for displaying his gladiatorship in that arena. On the other hand, mere lung force is despised'.[26] Some of those who came from more distant places had previously been in Gwennap circuit.

After 1900, most of the preachers were brought from across the Tamar and very few, apart from District Chairmen, from Cornish circuits. To name only a few of these (between 1907-26): Dr T. Ferrier Hulme the Warden of the New Room, Bristol in 1907[27] - it was from the New Room that Wesley had first set out for Cornwall), Charles W. Andrews (London, 1912) who spoke of his great grandfather having heard John Wesley preach in Gwennap Pit;[28] Dr Dinsdale T. Young (Kingsway Hall, London, 1913) who acknowleged (not in the Pit) the debt Methodism owed to the Oxford Movement and equally surprisingly gave his support to the deviation of British Israelism.[29] The preacher in 1926 was the young Isaac Foot the well known Liberal politician who was later to be a privy councillor and Vice President of the Methodist Conference.[30]

In the early years the preachers used the 'pulpit' marked by the two granite posts as one of them is seen doing in Trevena's drawing, but some of them liked to move to a place of their own choice, as Joseph Wood did in 1834.[31] An undated picture postcard of around 1905 shows the platform, consisting of four or five planks fixed together within an iron rail superstructure placed, on that occcasion, on the step immediately below the granite posts.[32]

v To Carharrack in the evening

The arrangements for the Whit Monday event were in the hands of the Gwennap Circuit superintendent minister and his helpers. A letter dated 6 June 1851 written by the Rev Joseph Spencer of Carharrack to the Rev Levi Waterhouse of Falmouth who was to preach in the Pit that year must have been typical of many, 'We fully expect you to be with us on Monday and shall be very glad to see Mrs Waterhouse with you. Mrs Henley wishes me to say that they will expect you to dine with them on that day...if it should be wet there will be services in the chapel, at the appointed hour, and you would be expected to preach in Carharrack chapel. We hope however to have a fine day...'[33]

The Pit Service in 1823 was held in the Carharrack chapel because of the bad weather, and this was to happen on a number of occasions over the years. The tea and evening meeting at Carharrack were held 'according to custom' in 1834. In that year however the Pit preacher was asked at the close of the afternoon service to preach again at Carharrack in the evening, which does not say much for the local arrangements![34]

Concert items were added in 1884.[35] The era of the popular lecture began, in 1913, when Dr Dinsdale Young of London spoke on 'People of Whom More Might Have Been Said'[36] and continued at least until 1950 when the Rev Frank T. Copplestone chose as his subject 'The defeat of Pessimism'.[37] The proceedings at Carharrack did not of course attract more than a segment of the afternoon congregation. At the end of that service the lanes around the Pit were crowded with pedestrians as well as vehicles and, as was once reported, 'hundreds tramped to Carharrack for the tea and meeting'. Quizzy described them as 'the more religiously inclined', others went to Redruth to catch the train or to visit the Fair,[38] and (for the 'religiously inclined') there were other events at Redruth Wesley and Redruth Fore Street churches. In 1871 John Ashworth, a popular speaker from Rochdale, who had addressed the congregation after the sermon at the Pit, was the speaker at a meeting at the Redruth 'Flowerpot Chapel' that evening.[39] In 1899 Matthew Clemens, the talented organist of the church, gave a recital on the organ which had been opened by Samuel Sebastian Wesley, and must have drawn a large number who might otherwise have been at Carharrack.[40] Rather surprisingly, in 1870, the Rev Samuel Coley, a well-known London minister, preached to a very large congregation at Redruth Wesley during the time of the Pit service itself.[41] Others, like the Blackwater schoolmaster, John Oates liked to finish off the day playing billiards in the town.[42]

vi A Musical People

The Methodists have always been known as a singing people and John Wesley made use of his brother's hymns, along with others, in the services which he conducted. Most of the singing heard in the Pit in the early days was unaccompanied and that must have been impressive. Wesley thought so, and commented, in 1775, 'No music is to be heard upon earth comparable to the sound of many thousand voices when they are all harmoniously joined together singing praises to God and the Lamb'.[43]

The first mention of music in the Pit was in 1838[44] and in almost identical words to those used by Wesley. Early references to particular hymns were in 1864 when the Rev Featherstone Kellatt announced 'Rock of Ages cleft for me' and in 1869 when the service began with 'Hymn 633 - 'Hail, thou once despised Jesus!'[45] In 1887 several innovations were made in the musical arrangements, the congregation that year was led by the united choirs of Truro, Carharrack and St Day accompanied by a cornet player. This was judged to be 'a wonderful improvement on former years'. The hymn sheets were printed for the first time and among the hymns used was 'Come Holy Ghost, our hearts inspire'.[46] These leaflets seem to have been reprinted each year, with the name of the preacher at the head until 1955 when it was decided to omit the preacher's name, presumably so that a stock could be built up for future use.[47]

In 1896 we read of 'musical selections', including solos, being included in the service. A stiff breeze was blowing from the north that day and the singing could be heard from a considerable distance away.[48] By 1901 community singing had been introduced for the half hour before the service began, and short addresses began to be used during that warm up time. The Truro coal merchant, 'Joey' Hunkin, addressed the company on one occasion.[49]

In 1907 the old order returned (if it had ever been completely abandoned) and the hymns were sung unaccompanied, in the old style - 'O for a thousand tongues to sing my great Redeemer's praise', 'Jesu lover of my soul', 'All hail the power of Jesu's name' and 'When I survey the wondrous cross'.[50] In 1911 the singing was led by two cornet players - 'an attraction to musical folks' it was said.[51]

vii A Cornish Pardon

The Cornish historian Mr A.K. Hamilton Jenkin, in a broadcast from the Pit in 1935, suggested that the Annual Service had the atmosphere of a Breton Pardon at which the sacred and the secular were intertwined, the religious service was also a social occasion. 'There was a striking parallel' he said 'between that assembly of Cornish Methodists and those of brother Celts in Catholic Brittany'.[52] In 1958 the Rev Edward Rogers of the Methodist Christian Citizenship Department made a similar suggestion when he told the congregation that, looking round on them, he detected 'a sense of a day out for most of those present'[53] - perhaps he noticed that some of them were eating ice cream wafers and cornets!

The Breton pardon, was a pilgrimage to a shrine culminating in a scene very much like that at Gwennap Pit. Writing about his childhood memories of the Folgoat Pardon around 1843, Douglas Sedgwick described 'the great day of the assumption of the Virgin at Folgoat' when vast numbers of people joined in what was both a holy day and a holiday. He travelled in 'a kind of omnibus behind which came the horses travelling gaily along the road'.[54] Another observer noticed the beggars swarming everywhere.[55]

So it was at the Pit - 'a sort of pious holiday' as the Gazette reported in 1838 and the scene was still the same thirty years later. In 1871 an observer noticed a procession of vehicles, 'large omnibuses to humble donkey carts following each other in quick succession in the direction of Busveal, on the road to which place dozens of blind men and cripples reaped a harvest from passers-by'.[56]

William Penaluna thought that most folk went to the Pit 'out of mere curiosity and for the fun of the thing'[57] and a report in the Gazette in 1842 says 'The attraction of the Pit never, within our remembrance, appeared to be greater, and no one could have gazed on that amphitheatre, crowded as it was in every part, and to its very brim, with so many thousands of people in cheerful holiday dresses, and have participated in the happy holiday proceedings which evidently pervaded the assembly, without considering himself well repaid for the journey he may have made to get there'.[58]

Substitute Gwennap Pit for Folgoat and the Methodist preacher between the granite posts for the statue of the Blessed Virgin and the general picture remains the same, as all the reports from the period suggest - the crowds, the vans, the horses, the catchpenny youngsters holding the bridles, the waggonettes and brakes, the donkey carts, the gingerbread, cake and other stalls, the holiday dresses, and the devotions - even the blind men and beggars 'making their dolorous appeals to the passing throng'[59]

On Whit Monday 1843 the recently formed Hayle Railway ran its first excursion train to Redruth for Gwennap Pit, 'that noted scene of Wesley's labours' and helped to swell the great congregation, vast numbers travelled by the new form of transport. 1,500 passengers arrived at Redruth station in four trains. On the last train leaving Redruth that day was a young man in a state of intoxication who fell from one of the open carriages on to the line where his hand was severed. It is not stated that the unfortunate man was a Methodist but a report made in 1864 makes the totally unexpected comment that 'the worshippers [on that occasion] managed to keep sober - an unusual circumstance'. This might be thought to be an uninformed if not also a malevolent comment, but Wesleyans were not all teetotallers, nor expected to be. On Whit Monday, 1844, a train leaving Hayle had difficulty in climbing an incline, stopped, paused, and then ran backwards. Some of the passengers took the risk of jumping from the carriages; others held to their seats and arrived back in Hayle shaken but unharmed! How many went on to Gwennap Pit we do not know.

In that year the Hayle Railway was taken into the newly formed Cornwall Railway (Truro-Penzance) and this in turn became part of the G.W.R. which was still advertising its transport to Gwennap Pit as late as 1914. At Helston station in 1910 hundreds booked for Redruth, many of them en route for the Pit.[60]

The photograph of the splatt behind the Pit (q.v.) probably dated c.1910, shows vehicles parked and a tent erected at the rear entrance to the Pit and people arriving from the direction of St Day. One report says the lanes became more and more blocked up by carriages and pedestrians. The traders put up their stands - stannins - on the splatt and others no doubt at the main entrance to the Pit. Perhaps they were successors to the solitary woman who is seen in Trevena's lithograph sitting at an empty table at the foot of the steps by the main entrance. Perhaps that was the bibles and testaments stand and perhaps she had just sold out.

The overflow of the congregation, and possibly also some of

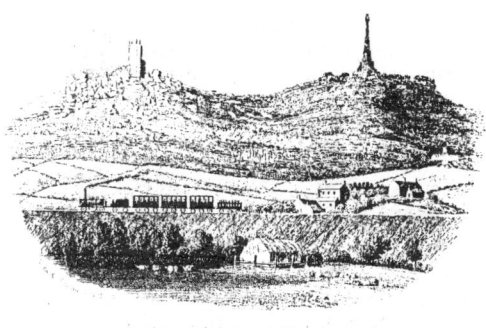

33

the stands outside the wall, found a place along the pathway that now leads to 'Rip van Laun'. In Wesley's time, of course, there were no containing walls. Ice cream vendors could still be seen on the splatt in the 1950s.

'Walking to the Pit' was a continuing feature of the Whit Monday scene right through the century. John Oates, the young schoolmaster from Blackwater, liked to walk to the Pit in the 1880s and '90s though in 1901 he went with 'Josiah Harper and his wife, Doo and I and four children in Tom Jenkin's Waggonette.'[61] In the 1950s motorists going through St Day to Busveal would pass many pedestrians on their way to the Pit. There were many more along Sparry Lane making their way from Redruth. One of the oldest people at the Pit service in 1948, eighty- six year old Mr G.H. Rowe, walked at least ten miles to and fro from Treleigh as he probably had done for years past.[62]

Mrs Ethel Escott of St Austell remembers that before she was three years old (around 1913) she was walked across the fields to the Pit from Mount Ambrose by her mother and nursemaid. She recalls from her childhood the long procession of people walking back to Redruth over the fields, often four abreast till they reached the stiles.[63]

And then there were the cyclists, among whom was Oswald Strongman, the organist at Nanpean, who cycled to the Pit in the 1930s, some fifty miles there and back, carrying a small bag containing two yeast buns for his lunch![64]

Children have always been interested in Gwennap Pit - it makes a splendid playground. Winifred Hawkey, in her Memories of a Redruth Childhood tells how her family made a ritual of walking to the Pit every Easter Saturday when the children could play, bouncing their balls up and down the terraces.[65]

It is evident from all reports that the Whit Monday pitgoers were not all Methodists; they came from all denominations and none - as they still do. In 1865 - 'After service in the Pit the great part of the congregation returned to Redruth, and their arrival was signalised by a sudden burst of unearthly noise from gongs, drums, speaking trumpets, organs, cymbals, &c...' Sanger's waxworks exhibition was there, and a mechanical gorilla, Daniel in the lions' den and - an effigy of John Wesley.[66] The Redruth pleasure fair grew rapidly between 1856-76 and in that last year 'Quizzy' gave his opinion that the Methodists who were then advertising the Pit Service more and more widely were responsible for bringing thousands of people into Redruth and into the fairground. 'All this' he wrote 'has grown out of the Pit'.[67] In 1882 the same writer opined that many people went to the Pit in the afternoon to get 'a snack of religion' before going into Redruth to laugh and romp.[68] He added, for good measure, that some of the Pit people who came into the

The Pit empty, (Valentine & Co.)
and full, early 1900s. (Royal Institution of Cornwall)

Two wartime Whit Monday Services: 1915 (Harvey) and 1917.

36

Edwardian Whit Monday
Photo: Govier, Chacewater.

Whit Monday on the Splatt
in the early 1900s.

37

Spring Bank Holiday Service 1973
Photo: Roskrow, Truro.

Holman-Climax Male Voice Choir, 1983
Photo: Parsons, Redruth.

town would read the posters posters with Scripture texts which the Town Missionary had put on the wall with one eye while peeping into the Fair meadow with the other. It was recognised that the pleasure Fair had been attracted to the town because of the thousands who came to the Pit each year,[69] while 'Quizzy', as we have seen, blamed the Methodists for inadvertantly publicising the event.[70]

WHIT MONDAY AT REDRUTH W3 *9th June, 1865.*

On Monday last, the usual service was held in Gwennap Pit, which was visited on this occasion by several thousands. After service in the Pit, the great part of the congregation returned to Redruth, and their arrival was sign. . . . The fair meadow was soon crowded by some five thousand people. . . . . There stood Sanger's waxworks exhibition, a highly creditable and extensive collection. There was also a performing mechanical gorilla, which spasmodically scraped a violin, and to borrow an old saw, grinned like a Cheshire cat; the Grecian Father and Daughter, an effigy of John Wesley; Moses and Company from the Sahara direct, with a questionable fluid said to be water running from the rock; Her Majesty and the Prince and Princess of Wales and all the Royal Family, who bow and move their corpse-like lips, but don't speak because it is not etiquette. The everlasting Daniel in the den of lions, and the Babylonian King out of harms way.

In 1887 'Quizzy' found that one or two baskets of oranges and ginger ale had found their way into the Pit and thought that many orange-rinds would be later be found on the seats of the sacred place.[72] It was the same twenty five years later. In 1906 'the vendors of fruit were present as usual', and, after another thirty years, in 1930s, as Mrs Escott of St Austell remembers, there was an ice cream cart and stall where you could buy juicy pears as you approached the main entrance to the Pit, and very desirable they were to small children.[73]

In 1866 it was thought by some that the stalls outside the walls were in too close proximity to the worshipping congregation.[74] In 1887 'Quizzy', the Redruth reporter, thought that the Pit was a medley on Whit Monday 'Within all was order, and devotional; without, all was jolly and secular'.[75] As late as 1958 the ice cream vendors were asked from the platform not to bring their wares for sale <u>within</u> the Pit.[76]

The contrast between the Pit congregations early in the century when the event was predominantly a religious affair and later in the century when it had become a religio-social occasion was commented on by a writer in the <u>Redruth Times and Camborne Chronicle</u> in 1869 who lamented the change and said that 'It is a pity that all persons who repair to the Pit are not actuated by the same motives as those which influenced our religious ancestors'. 'An old veteran' he said, remembered a service at the Pit in 1814 held during the Great Revival and said "It was heaven upon earth!" In those days, said the writer,'people went to get good; they were either religious people or anxious enquirers after salvation. There was not the dress, and giddiness, and frivolity that there is now. Now it is like Vanity Fair'. That, he thought, was the reason for the change, but improved means of travelling probably had something to do with it.[77]

39

viii Pictures and Postcards

The only picture purporting to show Gwennap Pit as Wesley knew it was an oil painting by the Bradford artist and engraver William Overend Geller (1804-81). The original canvas, 6' 6" x 4'8" seems to have been lost but fortunately Geller's engraving of the painting has often been reproduced and is well known; it is usually inscribed, with some variation, 'The Rev. J. Wesley preaching to Twenty-Five Thousand persons in the Gwennap Pit in its original state'. The picture however is far from showing the Pit in its original state!

Geller has been called a disciple of the artist John Martin who specialised in dramatic and apocryphal scenes, but a glance at Martin's canvas, 'Joshua commanding the sun to stand still' which shows the Israelite war leader standing to the left of a massive overhanging rock with two arms upraised, one holding a spear and the other in the attitude of prayer while many small figures of horsemen merge into the background will recognise immediately that in his 'John Wesley at Gwennap Pit' Geller was more than just a 'disciple' of Martin. He might be described as a plagiarist of Martin, for in his painting the great rock has become Wesley's pulpit, and Joshua with his arms upraised has become a woman engaged in prayer to the God of heaven. In Geller's picture Martin's warriors riding into the vale of Aijalon have become the serried ranks of Wesley's twenty-five thousand hearers at Gwennap Pit. Geller spent two years working on his canvas.[78]

In April 1845 the painting was exhibited in Cornwall, at the Wesleyan chapels at Lanner, St Day and St Mary's, Truro. The purpose of the exhibitions was to get subscriptions of 7/6d for copies of the engraving on India paper and 5/- for prints, 21" x 15", which would be delivered free of carriage during July or August. These prints found their way into Methodist homes and chapels throughout the country, and in large numbers in Cornwall. One can be seen in the Chapel at Gwennap Pit.

Less is known about F. Trevena [79] who was probably a Redruth man, certainly there was a family of that name in the town at that period. His lithograph of the Pit is as accurate as it appears curious, showing the crowded amphitheatre with a preacher, arm upraised, standing between the two granite posts. A number of people are walking along the top ring of the Pit and appear to be looking for places to sit, but without success, for even the gangways are filled with people. In the foreground a number of ladies and gentlemen stand around the entrance, a lady with a bonnet is sitting at a trestle table by the open gate, and on the left is a van bearing the name 'Albert', a name which in itself suggests the Prince Consort and the decade of the 1840s, a supposition which is supported by the dresses of the ladies in the foreground.

In 1887 'Quizzy' the Redruth correspondent of the Gazette

noticed that a photographer had climbed on to the roof of a cottage adjoining the Pit and set up his tripod close to a lime-washed chimney.[80] In 1896, when photographers were working from the same rooftop, the sun was shining brightly and from their viewpoint the Pit below seemed to be a mass of sunshades. After word was passed round the parasols were all lowered while two photographs were taken.[81] It is hardly possible that the 1887 photograph was the first to be taken in the Pit. The Redruth photographers Moody and Chenhall must have found 'the Pit empty' and 'the Pit full' to be a compelling Goyaesque subject. One photo of the full Pit by James Chenhall has survived.[82] By the end of the picture postcard era S.J. Govier, of Chacewater and other photographers had become familiar figures at the Pit.

Between 1902 and 1920 picture postcards were immensely popular and views of the Pit, usually of the crowded congregations were published year after year. It was a commercial enterprise and one Gwennap Pit card at least was printed as far away as Saxony.[83] Today these cards are eagerly collected. In them can be seen the faces of a multitude of now unknown people; very few can be identified - not even the man and woman on the top ring in 1918 though she marked their position and wrote on the back of the card - 'Dear Stan, Can you see father and I were the cross is'. Another card, posted at Scorrier on June 20th 1906 and addressed to Mrs Wenmoth, at the Ring of Bells, St Issey, is inscribed 'Hope you haven't one like this, would you like the Pit empty as well? Other cards contain scraps of information about other places than Gwennap, such as the one sent from 2 Park Villas, Ponsanooth, 1909, to Miss Lena Polkinghorne of Gwinear to inform her - 'We are having our harvest festival on Sunday...'

The men in the photographs tended to be bowler-hatted in the earliest scenes but for two decades after the Boer War the straw boater became ubiquitous. Umbrellas or parasols are often in evidence. Notice the ladies' summer attire in 1914, and the lady deep in thought on the front row. Notice the dog looking out from behind his master in 1917. Who were all these people? Who were the two prominent figures in close conversation, and the young people looking at the camera on the left of the picture; somebody's grandparents surely.[94]

ix Sunshine and Showers

The numbers attending the Whit Monday service continued to be impressive and were counted in 'thousands' though of course an accurate count was never possible A congregation of 4,000 was reported in 1925, 6,000 in 1929, 5,000 in 1932 and an estimated 10,000 in 1937, but in 1946 a congregation of nearly 3,000 was said to have been 'the largest for many years'. The estimate for 1950 was 6,000. The prevailing weather certainly affected the size of the congregation. There were much smaller attendances when the weather was bad, such as 1,500 in 1885 and 1,200 in 1935.

There were many fine sunny days, though the intense heat of 1871 and the 'blazing sun and cloudless sky' of 1929 were exceptional. It was the wet weather which made the headlines! In 1886 'a sudden heavy shower brought the service to an abrupt termination at the close of the sermon'.[85] In 1904 after a couple of hymns had been sung in the Pit, the service was adjourned to Carharrack for the first time within a decade.[86] On average, perhaps every sixth or seventh year, the weather was so bad that the venue was moved to Carharrack. It was held there in 1879, 1890, 1894 and 1904[87] What is more remarkable is that, for the most part, the services were held in the Pit rain or shine.

In 1885, in a Pit which was 'far from full', umbrellas and mackintoshes took the place of gay ribbons and parasoles'.[88] The postcard photographs of the congregations between 1900 and 1930 show parasoles in plenty - or were they umbrellas? The 1935 service was held in driving rain and soon there was a canopy of umbrellas over the Pit. No wonder the West Briton correspondent reflected 'What force but the compelling of a long tradition could have induced 1,200 people to leave their comfortable parlours and sit or stand for an hour in the driving rain?'[89] Rain and sleet greeted the Bishop of Truro in 1936. Lady Vyvyan, who was present, describes the 'sea of open umbrellas' 'the granite posts where a small microphone is swathed in a mackintosh', members of the congregation who have brought rugs and rubber-cushions, and the 'young girl with a Pekinese under her arm and the cape of her white mackintosh folded over her head'.[90] During a period of wet weather frogs have often been seen jumping about at the bottom of the Pit. Mrs Escott remembers a Whit Monday when a policeman went down through the congregation to pick up the frogs and carry them out.[91]

x   The Pit Renovation, 1936

Methodist Union, between Wesleyans, United Methodists and Primitive Methodists, came in 1932 after long years of division in Cornwall as elsewhere but it had been anticipated at Gwennap Pit in the previous year when the Rev Edwyn E Bennett, the popular minister of Redruth Fore Street Church (the United Methodist Free Churches, and later United Methodist, Conference Chapel) became the first non-Wesleyan Methodist minister to preach at the annual service.[92] Four years after Methodist Union Alderman George P. Dymond,M.A.,the headmaster of the Hoe Grammar School, Plymouth, a local preacher and Vice-President of the Methodist Conference was the preacher. He was the first former Bible Christian to stand in Wesley's pulpit.[93]

Certain circuit realignments took place at this time, and, in 1934, the Pit, along with Carharrack and Busveal, was transferred from the old Gwennap Wesleyan circuit to the newly amalgamated Redruth Circuit. The superintendent of the new Redruth circuit was James H. Watson and the minister at Carharrack was William Cooper, the former Primitive Methodist superintendent, who had moved there from his manse at St Day. Both Watson and Cooper took a personal interest in Gwennap Pit, the former was soon engaged on a renovation of the Pit and the latter was said to have written a history of Gwennap Pit.[94]

At the re-opening, in August 1936, Mr Watson presented the key to Mrs John Williams of Scorrier House and later expressed thanks to her husband, Major John Williams, (the great grandson of the 'King of Gwennap') whose interest and generosity had largely contributed to the success of the effort. Major Williams and his family were regular attenders at the Whit Monday service, when they occupied the 'squire's pew' to the left of the pulpit.

Speaking on the same occasion the superintendent said that although the Pit was now being called a Gwennap Memorial to Wesley it had, in fact, been a Wesley memorial since 1807. He further reported that the trustees had received a contribution towards the restoration from H.M. King George V, and another, unsolicited, from the Bishop of Truro.[95]

xi The Bishop, the Congregationalist and the Politician

The unnamed Bishop of Truro was Joseph Wellington Hunkin who had been enthroned in the previous year. He was no stranger to Gwennap Pit where his father, Joseph Weston Hunkin, a Methodist of 'the old type' sometimes led the singing, and where he had once addressed the congregation before the service proper began. The bishop had been a young local preacher in the Truro circuit, and for a short time, a Methodist minister before becoming an Anglican priest. There was a long wait also, and an uncomfortable one too, when Bishop Hunkin came to preach at the Pit on Whit Monday 1936. Rain and sleet were falling and a sea of umbrellas had been raised by those who possessed them by the time the Chairman of the District (Rev Frank H. Pritchard) and the Bishop entered the Pit. As the service continued Lady Vyvyan noticed that the people all around were singing heartily in the rain, knowing the hymns so well that they hardly needed to use the soggy hymnsheets which drooped in their hands. The Bishop preached on 'There be diversities of gifts but the same spirit.'[96]

In 1937 the Rev Dr. F.W. Norwood, the celebrated Congregational minister of the City Temple, London, preached in the Pit, another 'first' for it was the first time a nonconformist had preached in Gwennap Pit. He so impressed the congregation that he was invited to return again the following year, which he did.[97] In 1939, nearing the approach of war, Isaac Foot again preached in the Pit. With an eye on Hitler and Mussolini he said that the dictators were playing on the fears

43

of the people while in Britain there was much to instil fear, so we had our air raid precautions, bomb shelters and evacuations. But 'the answer to fear' said the preacher, was 'the Christian virtue of Hope'.[98]

Little was reported from the Pit during the war years but the annual services continued to be held, and in 1940, Dr Maldwyn Edwards, Methodist historian and biographer of the Wesleys, paid the first of his three visits to the Pit - he returned in 1965 and 1973.[99]

A number of amplifiers have been used in the Pit at least since 1935. In 1970 it was stated that the one then in use was causing concern. It is a useful instrument and one that Wesley would probably not have despised but there are still preachers and singers who feel that they can rely on the natural acoustics of the Pit.[100]

xii Protestant Incident

The rise of Anglo-Catholicism in the Church of England was clearly marked in Cornwall in the early decades of the present century. The attitude of the Methodists, ministers and laypeople, was not unlike that of the Cornish clergy to Wesley's ministry, some approved, a larger minority were hostile and the majority were indifferent. In 1932 the extreme practices of a devoted parish priest, Father Bernard Walke at St Hilary, raised Protestant fears and provoked a backlash of fury from the Kensitites of the Protestant Truth Society who physically wrecked his church. A year later a low Church layman, Mr W. Poynter Adams of St Minver prepared a grandiose scheme to form a League of Protestant Laymen to counter Anglo-Catholicism which could be launched in Cornwall. With the support of the Rev William Cooper, the superintendent of the St Day ex-Primitive Methodist Circuit, a rally was held in Gwennap Pit in August 1933, at which speeches were delivered by Sir John Haslam, M.P., Mr Harry Ould (a Helston Methodist and President of the Cornwall Free Church Council) and Mr Poynter Adams who produced letters of support from Maurice Petherick M.P., and two leading Methodist laymen, Isaac Foot M.P. and C. V. Thomas of Camborne. The rectors of Illogan and Landewednack also took part. Holman Male Voice Choir led the singing of hymns and two resolutions were unanimously adopted by the one thousand strong company, one to form a 'John Wesley and Henry Martyn Lodge of the Laymen of England League', and the other protesting against an alleged subterfuge which had coupled the Evangelical Revival with the Oxford Movement. After the rector of Landewednack had pronounced the Benediction it would appear that nothing further was heard about the League or the Lodge; at the end it was all a non-event. It was the only time that the Pit had been used for party purposes but the incident thereby became part of its history.[101]

xiii Music and Drama

The musical tradition of the Pit continued after Methodist Union and reports speak of massed choirs of the Redruth circuit, conducted by Mr J. Ivan Gill, the Lanner choirmaster and organist, the Carharrack and St Day Silver Band, conducted by Mr C. Allen and hymns being led by Mr Albert Merrin of St Day on his piano-accordian.[102] For some years in the 1940s the small chapel organ was carried into the Pit where it was played by Mr J. W. Martyn, the organist of Redruth Wesley.[103] In 1967 a united choir led by Camborne Town Band, was conducted by Mr F.J. Roberts[104]

In the 1950s and 60s, if not earlier, the organists of Busveal Chapel, Mrs Roberts, Mrs F. Veall and Mrs F.Phillips presided at the harmonium which was carried into the pit where it had its own platform.

Mrs F Veall and Mrs D Blackmore at the harmonium

A more modern musical style was introduced in 1969 when a Redruth Wesley youth group, 'The Pacesetters', sang hymns to modern settings with guitars and drums.[105] In 1975 a distinguished American choir, the Pfeiffer College Concert Choir of North Carolina, took part in the Pit Service. During recent years musical events in the Pit have ranged widely from Wesley and Sankey to Gospel Rock and Pop.[106]

The first mention of drama in the Pit was in 1949 when a pageant' described as 'The Wesleys in Cornwall' was presented at a District Youth Rally in the Pit.[107] It consisted of a number of linked scenes connected by a narrator, and seems to have led to the much more ambitious production of Christian Michell's 'The Wesley Tapestry' at the Pit during the Festival of Britain Year, 1951. It was ambitious because the cast of 120, mostly young Methodists, with little or no acting experience, had been brought together and rehearsed from many parts of Cornwall. The performance was widely acclaimed and was described by one critic as 'one of the most remarkable dramatic productions that Cornwall has ever seen'. Part of it was repeated at the Royal Festival Hall, London, in the following year. The part of John Wesley was played by the Rev Stainer Smith, of Truro, the Cornwall District Youth Secretary. The principal producer was Ivan Thomas of Newquay.[108]

In 1985 The Mystery Cycle, written and produced by John Sugden was presented by the Newquay Wesley Drama Group. There was a sweep of Bible history from the Creation to the Resurrection: The Lord God was seen sitting on the top rim of the Pit on the day of Creation and watching while Noah built his ark at the bottom. On one of the terraces of the Pit Jesus was teaching his disciples and along the steep passageways he carried his cross. In the same year the District Womens' Fellowship Pageant was held in the Pit and concluded with the release of a hundred balloons. A Charles Wesley 'Sing In' held during Wesley Year 1988 included a 'drama spot' in which John and Charles Wesley met in the Pit to discuss the forming of the first Cornish societies; then taking their leave of each other they went round the perimeter, until they met again, 'forty years later' to rejoice over the growth of Cornish Methodism.

Visiting parties have sometimes made their own drama spots: one day a group of Christian Endeavourers from 'up country' were seen doing an acted parable of God's control in which a small child wearing a mask (which apparently deceived every one but God!) crawled hand and foot around the Pit until he was stopped and his mask was removed, and it was discovered that he was not what he appeared to be; 'God looks not on the outward appearance but on the heart'.

One of the more unusual uses of the Pit over a number of years has been to use it as a footpath for sponsored walks on behalf of the Bible Society. To walk each circle of the Pit from top to bottom and back again is to walk one mile.

xiv   Trustees and Caretakers

In 1762 when Wesley first came to the Pit it was a holding in the Manor of Tolcarne [109] and may have been regarded locally as a no mans' land. So the people on the spot invited Wesley to make use of it on that occasion and presumably on his periodic visits over the next quarter of a century. Either after his death in 1791, or perhaps more likely in 1806 when the pit was remodelled 'with the lord's permision', a more formal arrangement was made, while at the same time, other open-air preachers, such as Rowland Hill, were able to use it.

In 1827 Joseph Entwisle enquired about the ownership of the Pit and was told that 'the amphitheatre is regarded by the lord of the manor as in the possession of the Methodists, and for their exclusive use'.[110] By 1838 the lords of the manor were the Duke of Buckingham and Charles Trelawney who held some tenements individually and some jointly. The Duke held 11/16th and Trelawney 5/16th of the Bosveal Pit tenement, of which Thomas Symons was the lessee and Mary Corner the occupant.[111]

Somewhere along the line a tenancy was obtained by the Methodists for in 1854 the Buckingham family's agent recorded that 11/- was due from the Methodist Society for two year's rent of 11/16th of Bosveal Pit to 25 March 1854.[112]

When it became possible, in 1936, to obtain a short lease of the Pit and Chapel from Scorrier House, a trust was formed and James H. Watson, the superintendent announced 'The whole has now been secured for Methodism'. Recognising that Gwennap Pit was significant for the whole of Cornish Methodism a representative 'Busveal Chapel and Gwennap Pit Trust' was formed, consisting of the superintendent minister, Col. J.E.T. Barbary, OBE, TD of Trevarth, Mr John Pethybridge JP of Bodmin, Mr J.C. Bickford-Smith of Trevarno, Mr Wallace C. Smith of Truro, Mr Donald W. Thomas of Camborne and Mr J. Eustice Wickett of Redruth. The lease was renewed at seven year intervals before the long hoped for freehold was obtained in 1978 and the link between the Pit and Scorrier House came to an end. In that year the site was sold off in lots by the Williams family and the trustees secured the Pit and Chapel with a defined area of ground around them.[113]

Following the passing of the Methodist Church Act of 1977 which affected all Methodist property, the trusteeship was vested in the Busveal Church Council, its members becoming managing trustees. This trust with a number of co-opted members, now generally referred to as the Gwennap Pit Committee, is the body at present responsible for the property.

Surprisingly when the 1936 trust was renewed in 1951 the District representation was not continued and a larger trust based largely on Redruth and Busveal members took over. The trust minutes, extant from 1951, reflect the continuing activity at the Pit over the last forty years, including the invitations to the annual preachers. They had a disappointment in 1955 when Dr Donald Soper's visit was cancelled at the last minute on account of a rail strike, and again in 1959 when Dr W.E. Sangster's eagerly anticipated visit could not be fulfilled because of his serious illness.

A succession of caretakers were employed over the years and given a number of duties to attend to, such as cleaning the chapel and keeping the grass cut. Mr and Mrs Blackmore recall the days when a horse was brought into the Pit to help keep the grass down but for the most part the caretaker and his wife were responsible for pushing the lawnmower along the half mile pathway; it was not until 1958 that a motor mower was introduced and the caretaker 'instructed how to use it. Since the last caretaker left the cottage Mr Blackmore himself has walked uncounted miles behind a mower circling the Pit in decreasing circles and earning for himself the title of 'the man who mows a mile of Methodism'. For forty years he has been 'our man on the spot' at the Pit and has kept a critical eye on the property and grounds and on the heating, lighting and general care of the Pit and chapel. All these things are recorded in the Minutes.

47

5 SPRING BANK HOLIDAY AND OTHER PIT EVENTS

i Finding God

With the change of Bank Holiday away from Whit Monday in 1967 the annual service was moved to the new date. The preacher that year was the Chairman of the District, the Rev R. Hubert Luke, who struck out for the depths by saying that 'no one living could prove the existence of God - a person had to take a leap of faith if God was to be found'. The Service was recorded by BBC TV and members of the great congregation were later able to see themselves on the screen - John Wesley's preacher had a much greater number of hearers throughout the country that day than ever Wesley himself could have imagined.'

There have now been twenty-five Spring Bank Holiday services though unfortunately too many writers of articles and compilers guide books still think the annual service is on Whit Monday. The wide range of preachers at those services have included one President of the Conference (Dr John Newton, 1982) and two Presidents Designate, Amos Creswell, (1983) and Ronald W.C. Hoar (1990). In 1973 the Rev Dr Maldwyn Edwards, Warden of the New Room and a past President, payed his third visit to the Pit.

ii Ecumenical

The Pit has been used for other than Methodist services from time to time. In July 1964 the Salvation Army South West Division held a Founder's Day Rally, which began with a Festival of Flags, in the Pit. In his address General Wilfred Kitching said that The Salvation Army was born in the womb of Methodism and they praised God for every evidence they had of close association and co-operation with Methodism.[2]

In 1977, the year of the Queen's Jubilee, the Scout and Guide movements celebrated their 70th and 60th anniversaries respectively, and the occasion was marked by a Sunday afternoon service conducted by Canon H.E. Hosking, the rector of Redruth.

The ecumenical climate of the time was evident at the annual service in 1982, after a decade which had seen the growth of ecumenism in the Cornwall, the Rev Dr John Newton (President of the Conference) was the preacher and Brother Michael, the Bishop of St Germans was present as an invited guest; both of them had returned from Canterbury Cathedral where they had shared in the visit of Pope John Paul a few days before; from Canterbury to Gwennap Pit an unforgetable experience and, as both of them remarked, 'a weekend of the Holy Spirit in our land'. In 1987 when the Cornwall Council of Churches annual service was held in the Pit: an address was given by Gerald Priestland, the well-known Quaker and Religious Affairs Correspondent of the BBC.³ Mrs Pat Griffiths, a leader of the Cornwall Quakers and the secretary of the Cornwall Council of Churches has said 'We look on Gwennap Pit as we do on the Cathedral as a place that belongs to all of us'.

Later in that ecumenical year Bishop Mumford, paid a pastoral visit to the parish, and went to the Pit with the Rural Dean where they were welcomed by the Rev Colin Allen.⁵

iii Roll Call

The exodus of Cornish miners to America, Australia, South Africa and other parts of the world in the last century was reflected in the formation of strong Cornish communities which are represented today in those countries by Old Cornwall societies and family reunions. Many of them took their Methodism with them and founded churches and Methodist dynasties there. It was to one such assembly that Mark Guy Pearse, on a lecture tour of America, announced that he himself had been a Cornish 'minor' for twenty-one years!

At Gwennap Pit it was noticed, at least from 1950, that the congregation at the annual service always included Americans, Canadians and Australians who were visiting their friends and relations in Cornwall, or trying to discover their roots in this mining countryside. The children and grandchildren of the emigrant miners - from America, Canada, Australia, South Africa and other places still visit the Pit on Spring Bank Holiday or during the summer months.

At the service in 1970 the Rev Tom Sanders, the circuit superintendent invited any visitors from overseas to come to the microphone if they so wished and say a word of greetings. Several of them did so, including Mr J. Williams of Detroit, and formerly of Camborne, the Rev W.B. Petherick, another Camborne man, who had spent over fifty years in Florida, Mrs E.A. Jays, of South Africa who had left Porthleven 64 years before.⁶ The emigrants were, of course, not all miners, Mr Vincent Cottell of Brisbane who visited the Pit in 1984 and belonged to an old farming family told us that his grandfather as a child had sung a solo in the Pit before his family emigrated to Australia. The Rev Edmund Warne and his wife of Wawona, California, have often visited the Pit. His ancestor of the same name was a farmer's son from near Truro who became one of the first Bible Christian ministers in this country - see the tablet in the chapel.

The custom which has developed of making a 'roll call' before the service starts still retains its interest even when it is extended to include England, Wales and Scotland, but it is interesting to see the mass of Cornish people in this Cornish pit, some of whom have been attending the annual service for many years. When Mr E.J. Brown, of Four Lanes, attended the annual service in 1959 it was reported that he had missed the service only twice over the past eighty years. He remembered walking to and fro from St Day to the Pit with his mother in the 1880s. His son, Gordon Brown, achieved a similar record before he died in 1991, and his grandson Ronald Brown continues the succession and is a member of the 'Pit Committee' today. Mr Stanley Brown, who was at the annual service in 1992, remembered singing a solo at a Sunday School event in the Pit in 1917.

iv Summer Services

Over two centuries the annual service has kept alive the original John Wesley preaching tradition: for a time during the 1930s it was supplemented by a Sunday afternoon service in the Pit. Since 1983 this service has been re-established during July and August each year concluding with a harvest festival. Special services have been held from time to time, including, in 1985, a service in the Cornish language at which the preacher was the Chaplain to the Cornish Gorseth, the Rev Frank Warnes. In 1991 a service was led by the Rev Herbert McGonigle of the Church of the Nazarene, and in 1989, 1990 and 1992, 'Sankey Services' were led by Mr R.C. Keast of Summercourt. In 1991 a 'Songs of Praise' programme was arranged by the Rev Richard Atkins of Newquay.

These services have usually been led by groups of Methodists from different Cornish circuits or from further afield. In Cornwall, Redruth, North Hill, Falmouth, Camborne, Bodmin, Helston, Launceston and Porthleven circuits might be named as well as circuit 'sections' and individual churches such as Tintagel, St Agnes, Newquay, Mylor, Troon, Whitemoor, Twelveheads, Nanpean, Penzance, St Keverne, Stithians, Lanner, Rosenannon, Carharrack, Chacewater, Threemilestone, St Ives, Roseland, and Bugle. Each group has conducted the service in its own style from the traditional to the modern. One circuit held the service for the reception of new local preachers in the Pit. Well-known music groups and soloists, including the Truro Praismakers, the Nankersey Quartette, the Goonhavern Quartette, the Kerensa Singers, St Newlyna Male Voice Choir and the Newquay Wesley Choir. Other churches have also helped including Truro and Redruth Baptist churches, Redruth, Camborne and Falmouth Salvation Army Corps, Frome Baptist church and, from Devon, Estover Methodist Church.

The Sunday afternoon services are well supported by summer visitors who have heard about Gwennap Pit and attract congregations of up to two hundred. Very often, as at the annual service, the congregation includes visitors from many parts of the world. Refreshments are available at the close of each service and some circuit groups have arrived early and picniced in the Pit. A set of photograph albums in the Visitor Centre prepared by Mrs Joan Shaw record some of these occasions.

6 BUSVEAL CHAPEL

i The Blacksmith and his sons

On the 17th July 1750 James Hitchens of Busveal, tinner, farmer, blacksmith and Methodist preacher made his sign with an 'X' on the draft of his will and this was witnessed by his friend James Bray.[1] He made bequests to his wife Julian, and to his children, William, James, Ebenezer, Mary, Sarah and Ann.

To his three sons he gave several portions of land in North Bosveal out of which they were to pay annuities to their mother and sisters, and in addition, James was to continue to let the 'society house' to the Methodist steward at the rent he was then paying and to be responsible for exterior repairs. Two elder sons of the blacksmith, Thomas and Samuel, had died before their father's will was made, but not before John Wesley had provided a niche for them in Methodist history.

Thomas, the eldest son (1723-46) worked at the tin stamps from the age of ten, and also helped in the management of his father's farm. He joined the Methodist society and, with his brother James, was a great help to them when the society house was pulled down by the mob and his father's house attacked. He died, and was buried on the 13th September 1746. John Wesley was at Gwennap (Busveal?) on the following day where he preached on 'For me to live is Christ, and to die is gain' so effectively that 'many of his hearers could not conceal their desire to go with him, and to be with Christ'

Samuel (1725-46) was converted by two of Wesley's preachers in 1744 and he became a vegetarian as an act of spiritual discipline. While tending to another preacher in his sickness, he caught the 'spotted fever' from which he died.

In 1744 the vicar of Gwennap reported to the bishop that there were Methodists in his parish and named James and Samuel Hitchens and Henry Uren whom he described as 'Methodist Public Teachers'. Charles Wesley met them in 1746 and accepted that they had been used by God but cautiously advised them 'not to stretch themselves beyond their line' and fancy themselves public teachers.[2]

William, the third son (1727-) was also a preacher though not named by the vicar, probably because he had just left home to join the band of Wesley's travelling preachers. Under Wesley's direction William Hitchens worked in some of Wesley's early circuits, (Cornwall then was one of them) and he was at Bristol, in the Midlands and in Yorkshire between 1745 and 1758. Busveal can then claim to have seen the beginning not only of Methodist local preaching but also of the Methodist ministry. These 'Early Methodist Preachers' lived spartan and heroic lives in the midst of much opposition.

William Hitchens was arrested and imprisoned at Bradford and would have been conscripted for the army if he had not been able to persuade the magistrates that he held a small estate in Cornwall jointly with his brother James. He was then given bail on a recognizance of £50 so that he could make the long journey home to collect his evidences. After four days rest at Busveal he returned to Bradford, with his documents and his brother James, where the case against him was dismissed. After twelve years he left the itinerancy, married, and settled in Bristol as a hatter.

James, the fourth son, (1733-) inherited his father's blacksmith's shop and, as we have seen, was given an interest in the society house. Ebenezer, (1735-), the youngest son, inherited the house at North Bosveal and looked after his mother.

ii The Early Society at Busveal

By 1767 there were sixty-three members in the Gwennap Society, which was centred at Carharrack, scattered around the parish, of whom fourteen, the largest concentration, were living at Busveal:[3] they were:

Julian Hitchens, widow, her son -
Ebenezer Hitchens, unmarried tinner
Ann Manly and her two sons
Henry and John Manly (tinners),
Mary Bray and her children, James (tinner) and Alice,
Temperance Bray, a widowed spinner,
Samuel and Phila (Philippa?) Jenkin
Robert Trewartha, tinner, and his wife Ann

The Trewarthas lived at Chengenter, (the mine later known as Cathedral Mine because it adjoined the Pit). Their daughter, Ann, later married William Bray of Twelveheads, and became the mother of William Trewartha Bray, better known as 'Billy Bray'.

The fact that fourteen Methodists were living at Busveal in 1767, and only five in Carharrack, suggests that a class would have met at Busveal and a society formed there (the usual sequence) long before the building of the present chapel. James Hitchens' society house was probably their first meeting place - the first Busveal 'chapel'. It is possible, of course, that although the family lived at Busveal the society house which they owned was at Carharrack and that that was where the Busveal members would have met and where the brothers defended the property from the attack of the mob. On the other hand it is reasonable to suppose that the society house which belonged to the Hitchens family, as early as 1750, was in fact at Busveal, but wherever the society house was there would have been, almost certainly, one or more earlier chapels in

52

succession at Busveal during the long period between 1767 and 1836 though no trace of them remains.

iii The 1836 Chapel

No account has survived of the opening of the present chapel.[4] Records of of the society are woefully lacking and it is only possible to give a sketchy account of its history. The Chapel and the Pit were in the Redruth Circuit until the formation of the Gwennap Wesleyan circuit. It finally returned to the Redruth Circuit following Methodist Union in 1932.

By the middle of the last century Sunday services were held at 10.30 a.m. and 6 p.m. and there was also a Monday evening meeting which was probably a preaching service. The two Sunday services continued for many years but the morning service had been discontinued by 1896 and the chapel ceased to be used for regular Sunday services a few years ago.

The congregation around, 1845. must have filled the small building to overflowing for William Francis, the Carharrack schoolmaster and versifier wrote of Busveal in that year:

Whene'er a Wesleyan approaches Busveal,
Pleasing thoughts of past times will o'er the mind steal;
Methodism in Gwennap, here, like a mere rill,
'Gan to flow, and to spread, and spreading is still;
A hundred and fifty do meet near the place,
Where Wesley to thousands oft' preach'd of free grace.

The attendance of 150 noted by Francis would have been based on a membership of around fifty in the mid-century.

Busveal society had a resident local preacher, S. Rickard, in 1854 and there were five, Messrs Tiddy, Brown, White, Nettle and Prater (the last two 'on trial') in 1864. Tiddy and Brown were also class leaders, together with a Mr Harris. A 1906/7 plan shows S. Rickard again (the same man?) as a resident local preacher. Harry Marks was the society steward in the 1930s.

The chapel makes no architectural pretensions; basically it is a square stone box with three windows on each of two sides; the original sash windows were replaced by plain glass with Gothic tracery, put in by the local firm of Vanstone and Bray in 1936 and, until 1990, a small entrance porch in which was a leaded window with coloured lights. Its furnishings are minimum: when it was opened in 1836 they probably consisted only of a small pulpit in the middle of the wall with leaders' and singers' seats on either side of it. A small communion table would have stood in the front of the pulpit.

Facing the front were two blocks of pews, one on either side of a central aisle, most of them being plain forms which were later boxed in. Considerable alterations to the interior were made in the 1880's (we would think) and in 1936. The Victorians, following contemporary fashion, removed the small pulpit and replaced it with a balustraded rostrum; they then placed a harmonium in front of it, dislodging the communion table which would then have been moved to the left hand side. The drawing by Mr Marks on page 57 shows the chapel as it then appeared, and as he remembers it, before the 1936 restoration. In that year the chapel was again rearranged and the rostrum replaced by a side pulpit constructed out of the old rostrum. The communion table was then returned to a central position but this time it was placed against the wall and fronted by a communion rail: the harmonium was moved to the left hand side. The organists at this period and later were Dolly Mitchell, Albert Merrin, Joyce Roberts, Doreen and Ruby Hooper. Mrs Campbell and Diane Veall.

The chapel was originally without decoration of any kind except, perhaps, a Geller engraving of John Wesley preaching in Gwennap Pit which may well have been introduced in 1845. At the centenary celebrations in 1936 Major Williams of Scorrier House presented a second copy of the engraving. The three framed portraits of Susanna Wesley and her two sons, John and Charles were later additions. In 1960 it was noticed that both Gellers were suffering severely from the damp and they were then backed with hardboard and rubber stops to limit the damage, but to little effect.

iv The Sunday School

The Sunday School was first mentioned in the 1830s and may have been formed before the present chapel was built. The purpose of the Sunday School in the earliest period was to teach the children reading and writing and introduce them to bible reading. Its anniversaries with their tea treats were among the highlights of the year, as they were in every chapel. The special services and the tea treats were usually held in the Pit, but the Round Field was also used. Both sites were conveniently at hand. Busveal Sunday School, headed by its banner and a hired band would parade to St Day and back at anniversary time. The procession, headed by its simple, but colourful banner, was preceded by the St Day and Carharrack Band. The route lay through Vogue and Scorrier Street and back along Telegraph Street to Vogue and Busveal.

In the 1930s the superintendent, who was also a local preacher, was Mr Jewell - he can be seen wearing a trilby hat in the postcard reproduced below - at that time there were fifty-two children in the school. Mr Jewell lived at Busveal and it is still remembered that he had a card hanging over the doorway of his living room bearing the words 'Faces not places make home'. He was succeeded as superintendent, in the 1940s, by Mr Harry Marks whose wife was the local postwoman.

Having no separate schoolroom the classes met in the chapel. We have a glimpse of the school in session one November afternoon in 1958 when two visitors from the Wirral opened the chapel door. A number of 'teen-age boys and some adults were in the back pew. Older girls and young children were sitting towards the front, and one girl was at the organ. Mrs Florence Veal, the superintendent, was standing at the front and a children's hymn was being sung. The visitors were shown to a pew underneath the Geller picture, and the school continued. They were told later that some of the older people present had joined the children that afternoon rather than attend the evening service because the weather was so rough.⁵

Illustration: R. Charles

Chapel Interior before 1936
as remembered by Mr T A Marks

50063 John Wesley's Chapel, Gwennap Pit, Redruth

57

7 PILGRIMS

i The Panels

The nine standing panels on the right at the approach to the Pit were placed there between 1983-86 to present the message of John Wesley, to show how his work spread through the world, and to tell the story of Gwennap Pit to all who pass by. The panels were designed by Clive Buckingham RIBA, and the wording on them was supplied by the present writer, but the actual building of the panels with all their artistry and mosaic was the creation of Guy Sanders of St Clement. It wasn't, the original intention that he should do more than the artistry and mosaic, but to help the work on at a difficult time, as he said, 'Guy Sanders the artist and mosaicist became also old Guy the mason'.

The line of panels begin with the preaching Wesley (based on Nathaniel Hone's portrait of Wesley in the National Portrait Gallery) and the congregation which surrounds him. These little figures serve a double purpose for they also represent by their style and dress, the countries around the world to which Wesley's Methodism spread. In that congregation is a self-portrait of the sculptor in his familiar beret holding aloft the figure of Charles Wesley which can be seen breaking the line of the top of the panel. Charles holds in his a hand a sheet of music, the score for the hymn 'O for a thousand tongues to sing...' The small figures crowd round the side of the panel towards the bright mosaic globe of the world in space. Under the globe are Edward Perronet's lines 'Crown Him ye morning stars of light' which lift the theme from that of Methodist expansion to the Joy of God's creation. The opposite panel presents a quotation from John Wesley in which he explains succinctly what he meant by his often quoted words 'The world is my parish'. The remaining panels show the Geller and Trevena engravings, while the last one, picking up the colourful mosaic of the Hone portrait and the globe, offers a simple 'Welcome' to all comers. The work did not proceed without delays, some of which were unavoidable. Guy's correspondence at the time conveys something of the frustration that he felt. The panels are a work of art and, because of that, are not equally understood or appreciated by everyone but Guy himself was encouraged when he visited the site 'in mufti' and overheard only appreciative comments. As far as he was concerned he had done the work to the glory of God. Sadly, he died within days of finishing the Panels and it is appropriate that a suitable space was later found to add a simple memorial to him in lettering around the circles of a Gwennap Pit motif.[1]

58

The Wesley Panels

Photos: George Langford

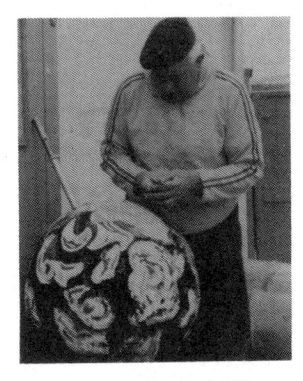

Guy Sanders
making the Globe

ii   The Visitor Centre

The Visitor Centre, like Rome, was not built in a day. The need for an extra room to be added to the Chapel had been evident for some time as more and more people found their way to the Pit and sometimes came in coachloads during the summer months. Parties from Treloyhan Manor Methodist Guild Holiday Home have been regular visitors for a number of years. Providing so many people with biscuits and cups of coffee which they could balance on their knees as they sat in the narrow pews became an increasingly hazardous occupation. Tourists like to find literature, souvenirs and postcards available at historic sites but there was no space at the chapel for more than a visitors' book. This service however was generously provided by Mr and Mrs Blackmore who turned the whole of the large porch in their cottage adjoining the Pit into a 'shop' while the Centre was being built.

In 1976 the Busveal Church Council launched an appeal to meet the cost of the purchase of the freehold of the Pit and Chapel. In the following year the treasurer reported that he held £1,853.09 including a grant of £500 from the County Council, and £900 had been promised. This appeal raised £3,278. In 1979 Clive Buckingham was appointed as architect and he prepared plans for a new building adjoining the Chapel and for a set of display panels at the entrance to the Pit.

A further appeal was launched in 1983 and over the next six years £20,922 was contributed. It was a splendid effort on the part of many people. The British Methodist Conference contributed £5,000 and eight other world Methodist conferences added a further £683. £750 was raised by Methodist Heritage Concerts organised by Mr W R Cocks of Launceston. Circuits, churches and individuals within Cornwall, and many from much farther afield sent donations, and over that period £6,574 was raised locally by sales and contributions at the Pit itself.

By 1983 the work was in the hands of the Manpower Services Commission and Guy Sanders the sculptor-mosaicist had begun work on the standing panels at the approach to the Pit. Unfortunately there were delays and not a few hitches in the building of the extension and the making of the panels but the foundation stones were laid (actually unveiled!) by Mr Bartlett Lang in 1987. In 1989 the MSC withdrew from the scheme and special arrangements had to be made for the work to be completed, but eventually the Chapel was restored and the Centre opened by Dr John Vickers in April 1991.

When the Centre was opened it became possible to offer a better service to our visitors. The coaches, mini-buses, cars, cyclists and pedestrians continued to arrive - Old Cornwall Societies, church groups and schools and many others, even an horticultural society. Since the opening day, the Centre has

Visitors from Treloyhan Manor
at the Centre

Indoor Panels

been staffed by a band of helpers, working on a rota, through the summer months, and that, we hope, will be the pattern through the coming years. The Centre includes an exhibition room and a shop, an open chapel in which to pause and pray and also toilet facilities. Here the visitor will find not only the tea or coffee and biscuits which they may require but also water for the dog's bowl outside. They will find sixteen panels of information about Wesley's World Parish today, (kindly supplied by the Methodist Church Overseas Division) bringing up to date the Wesley Panels outside. They will find literature not only about the Wesleys but about the missionary outreach of the Church, and also about local Methodism. Many visitors have gone on from the Pit to visit the Museum of Cornish Methodism at Carharrack.

iii The Chapel

Busveal chapel, with its very small membership, ceased to be used for regular services and then became, in effect, Gwennap Pit Chapel and part of the Visitor Centre. As such it is used as a chapel for prayer and meditation and occasionally for public services and other events. It was renovated in 1990 and reopened with pews from the closed Carnkie Higher chapel by Mrs Jeffery of Carnkie. At the Rededication Service a bust of John Wesley by Janet Stafford-Northcott, presented by the Rev Edmund and Mrs Nevo Warne of Wawona, California, was dedicated by the Rev Thomas Shaw in memory of Edmund Warne (1798-1828) Bible Christian minister and his wife Eliza, and also of Thomas Tregaskis of Hicks Mill (1785-1871) and his wife, both couples being among the forebears of the donor, four generations back.

In the chapel there is a set of photograph albums prepared by Joan Shaw, covering events in the Pit over the past nine years.

The Visitors' Book in the porch which has been in use since 1936 reads like a mini world gazetteer; many signatories are the descendants of Cornish miners who emigrated to America, Australia and other places in the last century. Some entries in it stand out for one reason or another - even a John Wesley signed his name recently!

iv Pilgrims

At Menheer, close to Gwennap Pit, is a Roman milestone marking an ancient road. According to a legend once well-known in these parts, similar to the story of the Christ Child at St Just in Roseland, St Paul came this way and stopped to preach at Creegbrawse. Medieval pilgrims certainly passed by as they went from St Day to St Michael's Mount.

Since John Wesley's last visit to the Pit, in 1789, Gwennap Pit has been on the Wesley Trail. Many pilgrims and countless visitors have made their way here. Implicit in the decision made in 1806 to make the Pit a memorial 'in memory of Mr Wesley' is the recognition that it is a special place always to be associated with his apostolic work.

During the Wesleyan Conference at Camborne in 1862 John Rattenbury, the retiring president, finished his year of office by going to preach at the Pit during the Conference sessions. He wrote afterwards 'It was a noble thing to be able to finish my presidency at the Gwennap Pit, standing where Mr Wesley stood. The Lord has been very good'.[2] Dr Leslie Newman who preached at the Pit in 1966 went further and said that outside of Palestine he had never worshipped in a place which had moved him quite so much - 'I can almost hear the clatter of John Wesley's little pony coming down the lane yonder'. A recent preacher prostrated himself in papal manner at the site. Others have called it a shrine and 'a sacred spot'.[3]

Edward White Benson, the first Bishop of Truro and later to be Archbishop of Canterbury, rode out to the Pit with his young son Martin to show him 'glorious old John's preaching place' and to pray over it in a downpour of rain.[4] Bishop Mumford called at the Pit during a pastoral visit to the parish in 1982, thought of John Wesley, and posed by the granite posts with upraised arm. All these were pilgrims.

There are a hundred places in Cornwall where we can walk in Wesley's footsteps but first among them must be Digory Isbell's cottage at Trewint on Bodmin Moor, where we can look into the little rooms and, in our imagination, see him seated at the table writing to his correspondents, and then reading his Bible by the light of a candle before getting into bed - and - Gwennap Pit in which year after year he made his message known to vast crowds of tinners and their families, and perhaps announcing to the crowd of miners and their famlies that hymn of his brother's which the first panel still announces to every pilgrim who comes this way today:

> O let me commend my Saviour to you,
> I set to my seal that Jesus is true.

Sunday Service in the Pit

Leaving the Pit after the service.

1 THE SCARRED LANDSCAPE

1. Later called Cathedral Mine because of its proximity to the Pit. For the name Jengenter (Chengenter) see D.B. Barton, Essays in Cornish Mining History, I (1968) p. 106.
The name Chengenter (p.176), or Jengenter is probably a corruption of a Cornish form, i.e- Chy-an-Kenter, the house by the wedged-shaped valley.

2. WB 16 Oct 1986.

3. The Cornish Banner

4. The Wesleys in Cornwall, John Pearce, Barton, Truro, 1964, pp.138f., 147, 152

5. Memoirs of Rev Thomas Wills, by A.B., pp. 40, 54

6. RIC/Thurston Peter Coll. 8/7

7. Gazetteer of Cornwall, R. R Symons, Penzance 1884, p. 141;
Minerologia Cornubiensis, W Pryce, (1778) p. 141.

8. It was succeeded by an octagonal chapel in 1768 and by the present church in 1815, all of them probably on the the same site.

9. The Wesleys in Cornwall, John Pearce, D.B. Barton, Truro, 1964, p 44; An Epistle to the Reverend Mr John Wesley, by Charles Wesley, Presbyter of the Church of England, London, 1755, p. 15f.

10. Ibid p. 44

11. Ibid p. 59. The word 'sinners' is not a misprint for 'tinners', which they were, but an allusion to Zacchaeus in St Luke's Gospel. 19: 7,9.

JOHN WESLEY'S AMPHITHEATRE 1762 - 1789

1. There are a number of editions of John Wesley's Journal. The Bicentenary edition of 1938, in eight volumes, contains, in addition to the Journal the diary where extant, from which it was written up. For Wesley's Cornish journeys, the single volume The Wesleys in Cornwall, John Pearce, (Bradford Barton, Truro 1964) is convenient to use and although it doesn't contain the diary, it does have John Pearce's invaluable footnotes and the further advantage of including also the Cornish journals of Charles Wesley and John Newton.

On four of Wesley's visits to Gwennap after 1762 the Pit is not specifically named as his preaching place but that it was can be inferred from the context. The case of his 1765 visit is rather different, and it has been suggested that Wesley may on that occasion have reverted to his earlier preaching site 'in the plain' at Carharrack (see The Christian Miscellany 1868 p. 19), but that seems hardly likely.

65

2 Methodist Societies Book (1785-1796) CRO/MR/

3 The word 'prayers' in the diary normally means morning or evening prayer at the parish church.

4 There is no clear evidence of a society at Busveal at this date. Wesley mentioned a society meeting being held following the Pit service in 1778, 1785 and 1789, but these could have been held at Carharrack.

5 *A Family of Cornish Engineers, 1740-1810*, F.B. Michell, Trevithick Society, 1984, p. 33.

6 *The Letters of the Rev John Wesley*, A.M. Ed. John Telford, vi 68, 76. *The Works of the Rev. John Wesley*, iv 261-64.

7 *The Wesleys in Cornwall*, John Pearce, D. Bradford Barton, Truro, 1964, p. 156

8 Ibid p. 142; Wesley Letters iv 311

9 *Letters of John Wesley; A Family Record*, Enid Smith

10 *Camborne Wesleyan Circuit Magazine*, No. 6 (June 1889), 'Extracts from Captain James Thomas' Diary'.

11 *An Historical Survey of the County of Cornwall*, A new edition Helston I 1848, printed and published by W. Penaluna, p. 237.

12 *The Wesleys in Cornwall*, John Pearce, D. Bradford Barton, Truro, 1964, p. 155. *Letters of John Wesley*, vii 112

13 MS Diary of Richard Treffry, 10 Oct 1802.

14 *Foolish Dick, An Autobiography of Richard Hampton, The Cornish, Pilgrim Preacher*, S.W.Christophers, London, Haughton & Co [1873], p.

15 *History of Wesleyan Methodism* George Smith, ii, 264; WB 8 Jun 1871

16 Diary of Anna Reynalds of Truro, 4 March 1831 CRO/ , RIC/ShawColl/ transcript p. 113.

17 *Long Life and Peace, Memorials of Mrs Elizabeth Shaw...* R.C, Barratt, London 1875, p. 15

18 *History of Wesleyan Methodism*, George Smith, II, p. 264?

19 *Early Methodist Preachers* 1838 Edn pp 378-80. Taylor was told that 'it was sure to be a fair day when there is to be preaching in the pit' but it is clear from his account that, like Wesley, he was at the Pit on the Sunday.

20 Diary of Richard Treffry, 10 Oct. 1802

21 *Memoirs of Rev Thomas Wills*, by A.B., pp. 40, 54ff Selina, Countess of Huntingdon, established a little Methodism of her own and employed her own travelling preachers. She gave some support to Wesley but much more to George Whitefield and the Calvinists. Her 'Connexion' in which Wills became a minister, used the Anglican liturgy but eventually, and for the most part, joined the

Congregational Union. The Calvinists believed in the salvation of God's elect whereas Wesley was an Arminian, teaching that salvation was the free gift of God for all who would accept it. Both doctrines can be found in the Anglican prayer book and in the Bible.

22 Gospel preachers - Calvinist preachers. Wesley saw the work of the Calvinists as a threat to his own work in Cornwall and strongly criticised them.

23 We have not been able to find any evidence of a Calvinist chapel of any description anywhere near Busveal.

24 Excepting on Wesley's visits!

25 The students were ministers-in-training at Lady Huntingdon's theological college at Trevecca in South Wales.

26 The Enthusiasm of the Methodists and Papists Compared, Richard Polwhele (London 1820), p. ccxcviii, Revival Cameos, P.W. Gentry, (Pershore 1985) pp. 27-32.

3 THE PIT REMODELLED

1 Essays in Cornish Mining History, D.B.Barton, ii 14f.; Mining Journal 8 and 15 Mar 1879, 6 Jun 1885; RIC/Cornish News Cuttings/ 5/SJ Wills;

2 Gaz 20 May 1826.

3 Cornubian 30 Jun 1871.

4 RIC/Thurston Peter Coll. 8/7

5 Michell, A Family of Cornish Engineers, 1740 - 1910, F. Bice Michell, p. 33. The Trevithick Society, 1984. A later writer has added to the the Memorandum the words, 'Richard Michell, Steam engineer'.

6 RIC/Thurston Peter Coll. 8/7

7 Old Cornwall. X No. 12 (1991) pp. 594-98 'Gwennap Pit and its Origins', M. Tangye. The sketch plan was passed down through the Michell family and was recently copied by Mr Michael Tangye of the Redruth Old Cornwall Society for preservation in the Society's archives, and used in his article in Old Cornwall.
Mr Tangye makes good use of Richard Michell's account but it should be noted that Mrs Skinner's 'memories' of Wesley at the churchtown and of his later finding the Pit are at variance with Wesley's own account of his finding the Pit in 1762. There is no evidence that Wesley preached at the Churchtown.

The first of the 'principal subscribers' on Michell's list looks like 'Jno Willer Esqr'(or Miller) but Michell abbreviates some of his words, such as 'Jenky' for Jenkyn, 'princip' for principal, and 'Jno Willer Esqre', should be read 'Jno Willm Esqr' - as we would have expected, John Williams of Scorrier House.

8 The Trevena print first appeared in Views of Cornwall, Rock, London and is

67

inscribed 'F. Trevena del Rock & Co.sc No 318' The book contains about thirty illustrations dated between 1830 and 1852.
There were Trevenas in Redruth at that period including a Francis Trevena in 1799.

9   History and Description of the Town and Harbour of Falmouth, Richard Thomas, (Falmouth, 1827), p. 146f.

10 Memoir of the Rev. Joseph Entwisle, fifty-four years a Wesleyan Minister, Joseph Entwisle, 2nd Edn. Mason 1854, p. 348

11 The Life of the Rev Joseph Wood, H.W. Williams (1871)

12 Falmouth Express   6 Jun 1838

13 These Things Have Been, Richard R. Blewett, 28th Instalment, August 1966; Western Morning News 3 Jun 3 Jun 1966.

4   WHIT MONDAY AT THE PIT

1   RIC/Thurston Peter Coll/8/7

2   Gaz 11 Jun 1808

3   Gaz 20 May 1809   exhort

4   Gaz 20 May 1814 C.C. James in his History of Gwennap, p. 55, p.55 is no doubt right in surmising that Whit Monday was probably chosen for the annual service to counteract the revelry and hard drinking at Gwennap parish feast.

5   Ibid For Treffry see Richard Treffry Senior, Thomas Shaw, CMHA Occ Pub 1969.

6   Gaz 24 May 1817

7   Gaz 2 Jun 1821

8   Gaz 24 May 1823

9   Gaz 21 & 28 May 1825

10 The Enthusiasm of Methodists and Papists Considered, by Bishop Lavington, with Notes by the Rev Richard Polwhele, Vicar of Manaccan and St Anthony, p. ccxcviii footnote (London 1820); WB 27 Aug 1819. For Hill see also Bibliotheca Cornubiensis I, 240; Revival Cameos, P.W. Gentry, Pershore, 1985, pp. 27-32

11 WB 2 Jun 1843, 'Wesleyan Missions' and advertisement.

12 Gaz 10 Jul 1940

13 Memoir of the Rev. Joseph Entwisle, fifty-four years a Wesleyan Minister, by his son, 2nd Edn. Mason 1854, p. 348

14 Primitive Methodist Magazine, 1833, p. 20

15 Samuel Dunn, 1798-1882, T.R. Harris Cornish Methodist Historical Association Occasional Publication No. 6 (1963).

16 Memorials of Thomas Garland of Fairfield, Redruth, London, 1868, pp. 355ff.

17 'Address of the Radical Reformers meeting at Gwennap Pit 1839', John Carne, B Lib Add. MSS 34245, Folio 178 - Photpcopy, RIC.

18 For this event or non-event see: Gaz 5 Apr 1839; WB 5 Apr 1839; JRIC New Series IX pt 1, p. 60; 'Cornish

Methodism and the Chartists', M.S. Edwards, CMHA Journal II 109f, 134f.

19 Gaz 28 Jun 1839

20 Gaz 3 Sep 1886, see also Gaz 12 Aug 1887

21 Gaz 19 May 1834; The Life Rev Joseph Wood, H.W. Williams (Wesleyan Conference Office, 1871), p. 97f.

22 Memorials of the Rev John Rattenbury, ed H.O. Rattenbury, 2nd edn. 1884, p. 57

23 Gaz 20 May 1864

24 Gaz 10 Jun 1876

25 Gaz 17 May 1888

26 Gaz 30 May 1884

27 Gaz 23 May 1907

28 Gaz 5 May 1912

29 Gaz 15 May 1913

30 Gaz 19 May 1926

31 Christian Miscellany, xiv (1868) p 18

32 RIC/Shaw Coll/PCs

33 MARC/MAM/PLP/98/9/6

34 The Life of the Rev Joseph Wood, H.W. Williams (Wesleyan Conference Office, 1871), p.97f.

35 Gaz 6 Jun 1884

36 Gaz 15 May 1913

37 Methodist Recorder, 1 Jun 1950; Gaz 31 May 1950

38 Gaz 28 May 1880; Cornubian 21 May 1869

39 Gaz 2 Jun 1871

40 Gaz 25 May 1899

41 Gaz 11 Jun 1870

42 Diary of John Oates

43 JWJ 3 Sep 1775

44 Gaz 6 Jun 1838

45 Gaz 20 May 1864; Cornubian 21 May 1869

46 Gaz 3 Jun 1887

47 Trust Meeting Minutes, 17 Feb 1955

48 Gaz 28 May 1896

49 Gaz 30 May 1901

50 Gaz 23 May 1907

51 Gaz 8 Jun 1911

52 WB 13 May 1935; Gaz 12 Jun 1935 &c

53 Camborne-Redruth Packet 28 May 1958

54 A Childhood in Brittany Eighty Years Ago, Douglas Sedgwick, 1919

55 The Land of Pardons, A. Le Braz, 4th edn. 1912, p. xviii

56 Gaz 6 Jun 1838; Cornubian 2 Jun 1871

57 An Historical Survey of the County of Cornwall, A New Edition, Helston, 1848, printed and published by W. Penaluna, p. 237

58 See Gaz 20 May 1842

59 There are many references in the press to the 'Pardon' atmosphere of the Pit up to the end of the century; e.g. Gaz 6 Jun 1838, 20 May 1842, 10 Jun 1876, 2 Jun 1882, 3 Jun 1887, W.B. 9 Jun 1843 20 May 1853, 9 Jun 1865

60 Woodfin, R.J. The Cornwall Railway, p.1.; Anthony, G.H. The Hayle, West Cornwall and Helston Railways, Oakwood Press, 1968; WB 9 Jun 1843, 20 May 1853; Gaz 16 May 1845; Cornubian 2 Jun 187; Gaz 19 May 1901; Handbill dated Paddington, May 1914

61 Diary of John Oates, 17 May 1880, 1882, 22 May 1899

62 WB 20 May 1948

63 Letter to the writer from Mrs Ethel Escott (nee Tredinnick).

64 Per Mr W.C. Brenton, Nanpean

65 Memories of a Redruth Childhood, Winifred Hawkey Dyllansow Truran (1987) p. 52f.

66 WB 9 Jun 1865

67 Gaz 10 Jun 1876; Cornubian 21 May 1869, p. 3

68 Gaz 2 Jun 1882

69 Cornubian 21 May 1869 p. 3.

70 Gaz 10 Jun 1876

72 Gaz 27 May and 3 Jun 1887

73 Letter to the writer from Mrs Ethel Escott (nee Tredinnick).

74 Gaz 24 May 1866

75 Gaz 3 Jun 1887

76 Camborne-Redruth Packet 28 May 1958

77 Redruth Times and Camborne Chronicle 21 May 1869, p. 3

78 Bradford Antiquary, 1894, p. 4ff.; Wesleyan Methodist Magazine, 1908, p. 410; Gaz 18 Apr 1845; RIC/Shaw RIC/Shaw Coll/Gwennap Pit.

79 Trevena's drawing appeared in in Rock & Co's Views of Cornwall which was published in London in 1852. The book contains a number of lithographs dated between 1838 and 1852. The Trevena drawing is not dated but its early serial number suggests that it was made in the 1840s. Another lithograph (which may also be Trevena's work) shows the de Dunstanville monument and though it is neither dated nor signed must have been made after the raising of the monument in 1838 and before the publication of the book in 1852. This delightful picture, which shows a train with its tall chimney passing by Carn Brea, can therefore be dated to the lifetime of the Hayle Railway, 1838-52 and the train must be one of those described in the Gazette, in 1843, as providing 'so convenient and speedy a conveyance for visiting Gwennap Pit'. Redruth was the nearest station and from there the passengers either walked or travelled to the Pit in the 'Albert' and similar vans.

80 Gaz 3 Jun 1887

81 Gaz 28 May 1896

70

82 Views and Likenesses, Charles Thomas (R.I.C. 1988), p. 43; RIC/Shaw Coll/Gwennap Pit

83 Old Picture Postcards of Cornwall, Sara Paston-Williams, Bossiney Books, 1989, pp. 4ff. For examples see RIC/Shaw Coll/Gwennap Pit.

84 RIC/Shaw Coll/ Gwennap Pit

85 Gaz 18 Jun 1886

86 WB 26 May 1904

87 British Association Guide to Redruth p. 14

88 Gaz 29 May 1885

89 WB 13 Jun 1935;

90 Our Cornwall, C.C. Vyvyan (1948) pp 94-101;

91 Letter to the writer from Mrs Ethel Escott (nee Tredinnick

92 WB 28 May 1931

93 Gaz 22 May & 12 Jun 1935; WB 23 May & 13 Jun 1935

94 Gaz 22 May 1935

95 Gaz 2 Sep 1936; WB 20 May 1948

96 Gaz 3 Jun and 10 Jun 1936; Our Cornwall Lady Vyvyan 94-101

97 Gaz 19 May 1937; 8 Jun 1938

98 Gaz 31 May 1939

99 Gaz 22 May 1940

100 Gaz 12 Jun 1935

101 Gaz 16 Aug 1933, WB 17 Aug 1933

102 Gaz 22 May, 12 Jun 1935; 3 Jun 1936

103 WB 20 May 1948

104 WB 1 Jun 1967

105 WB 29 May 1969, 28 May 1970

106 WMN 28 May 1975

107 Gaz 23 Jun 1949; 'The Wesleys in Cornwall' (Play)

108 WB 23, 26 Jul 1951; CP 11 Aug 1951 The Wesley Tapestry

109 A History of the Parish of Gwennap, C.C. James, p. 71

110 Memoir of the Rev. Joseph Entwisle, fifty-four years a Wesleyan Minister, by his Son, 2nd Edn. Mason 1854, p. 348

111 Gwennap Tithe Map, 1838

112 RIC/A. Jenkin Letter Book 1854.

113 See WB 20 May 1948 etc

5 SPRING BANK HOLIDAY

1 WB 1 Jun 1967
2 WB 9 Jul 1964 p. 7
3 Chronicle 20 (Harvest 1987),
4 WB 3 Jun 1982
5 WB 11 Nov 1982
6 WB 28 May 1970
7 Gaz 21 May 1959;
8 Meth. Rec. 13 Jun 1991

6 BUSVEAL

1 For the Hitchens family see: Will of James Hitchens of Gwennap, tinner, 1752, CRO;

71

The Wesleys in Cornwall,
John Pearce, D. Bradford
Barton, Truro, 1964,
pp. 51f., 96;
Gwennap Registers 1658-1786,
transcribed by W.L. Bawden.
Episcopal Visitations,
Gwennap Parish.
THOMAS HITCHENS: The Wesleys
in Cornwall, John Pearce, D.
Bradford Barton, Truro, 1964,
p. 96, 98; WILLIAM HITCHENS;
John Wesley's Works, ii, 226,
393f,
Letter from Hitchens to John
Wesley about his arrest at
Bradford, dated 28 Feb 1767,
Wesley's Works, xiii 341f;
John Wesley and the Advance
of Methodism, J.S. Simon,
Epworth Press (1925) p. 250;
Hitchens at Leeds Conference;
The Wesleys in Cornwall,
John Pearce, pp 52, 96;
Methodist Memorial, Charles
Atmore, (1801), p. 190

2 The Wesleys in Cornwall,
John Pearce,
D. Bradford Barton, Truro,
1964, pp. 51f.

3 West Cornwall Circuit
Membership Lists, June/July
1767, CRO/
Photocopy and Typescript copy
with Index, Shaw Coll./RIC.

4 The date '1836' is based on
the chapel's centenary,
celebrated in 1936, but an
earlier date, 1833, is
possible (See Stat. Returns.)

5 Methodist Magazine, Aug 1959

7 PILGRIMS

1 Gwennap Pit Wesley Panels,
pp. 8 including 'The
Sculptured Figures' by
Guy Sanders; Frank Wintle's
Helena Sanders and the Cats
of Venice, Souvenir Press
1989, pp. 196-98 gives an
interesting account of the
'frustrations' but it should
be read in the light of the
Sanders' correspondence -
RIC/Shaw Coll/Sanders.

2 Memorials of the Rev John
Rattenbury, Ed H.O.
Rattenbury,
2nd Edn 1884, p. 57

3 W.B. 2 Jun 1966

4 The Wesleys in Cornwall, John
Pearce, Truro 1964, p. 26

5 W.B. 11 Nov 1982